NEVILLE SOUTHALL

WITH RIC GEORGE

IN SEARCH OF PERFECTION

B&W PUBLISHING · EDINBURGH

First published 1995
by B&W Publishing
Edinburgh

ISBN 1 873631 59 6

A catalogue reference is available from
the British Library.

Picture Credits: The publisher would like to thank
the following for their kind permission to use the
photographs on the pages listed. All photographs
are copyright.
Action Plus: pages 21, 59 and cover photo.
Allsport UK Ltd: pages 4, 7, 11, 15, 17 and 43.
Coloursport: pages 2, 10, 31, 40, 47, 64 and 67.
Steve Hale Photography: pages 13, 18, 20, 23, 33,
53, 62, 65 and all the training photos.
Steve Lindsell: page 29.

ACKNOWLEDGEMENTS

I would like to thank the following:

Ric George for his work in putting this book together
Jimmy Gabriel for his ideas, input and enthusiasm
Steve Hale for his photographs
Paula Cox for the graphics
Peter McIntosh (A.C.K. printers, stationers and
office furniture suppliers, Liverpool) for his backing
Jason Kearton, Stephen Reeves, James Speare
and Richard Moore for their availability and patience

Neville Southall

CONTENTS

FACT FILE

BIRTHPLACE: Llandudno, Wales

BIRTHDATE: 16th September 1958

HEIGHT: 6' 1"

WEIGHT: 14st 7lb

CLUBS PLAYED FOR: Winsford United, Bury, Port Vale (loan), Everton.

PREVIOUS JOBS:
Labourer, chef, hod-carrier, binman, and hod carrier again.

EVERTON APPEARANCES:
By the start of the 1995/96 season, I had made 494 league appearances (650 in all competitions), beating Ted Sagar's previous record of 463. This includes a record 35 Merseyside derby appearances.

HONOURS:
Two League Championships (1985, 1987), two FA Cups (1984, 1995), one European Cup Winners' Cup (1985) and one Football Writers' Footballer of the Year award (1985)

FULL INTERNATIONAL CAPS:
81—a Welsh record.

EVERTON DEBUT:
Against Ipswich on October 17th 1981 in a 2-1 victory at Goodison Park.

WALES DEBUT:
Against Northern Ireland at Wrexham on May 27th 1982. Wales won 3-0.

MOST DIFFICULT OPPONENTS:
The Everton back four!

GREATEST SAVE:
Against Tottenham's Mark Falco at White Hart Lane in 1985. It helped us win a crucial league match and we went on to become champions.

GOALS SCORED:
One. In a penalty shoot-out against Charlton in a Full Members cup-tie at Goodison Park. I know nobody else counts it—but you try taking it away from me!

FOREWORD

Neville Southall is the prime example of someone who has combined natural talent with sheer diligence to reach the top of his profession. It is a testimony to his determination and ambition that he has achieved the incredible transformation from a modest Llandudno hod carrier to a record-breaker for both club and country. Moreover, he deserves further credit for continually striving to improve on a level of which almost every other goalkeeper would be justifiably proud. I have seen enough of Neville in training and in matches to recognise that he is something special

I first met Nev when I joined the Everton coaching staff in July 1990. Since I've known him, I have marvelled at his mental and physical courage, his professionalism, plus his all-round ability as he strives to be the best. It has been my privilege to witness his patience and kindness to people who ask him for tips or simply his autograph. Such is his love for his job that when Everton visited Ireland a few years ago, Neville took the opportunity to organise a free coaching clinic for youngsters in the Dublin area. That's typical of him.

As he would tell you, he is not the finished article, but I believe he is the nearest thing a keeper can be to it. It is that rare and precious ability which convinces me that this book, featuring Nev's experiences and tips, and written in his usual forthright manner, will prove invaluable to all keepers of all ages, male and female. After all, if you use Neville Southall as your role model, then you can't go far wrong. His is a coaching manual like no other, for it not only illustrates ways of improving technique, it also stresses that whatever gifts you have, they will not be exploited without hard work. And there is no harder worker than Neville Southall.

JIMMY GABRIEL

1

INTRODUCTION

So you want to be a goalkeeper? Well, that's unusual. Do you remember at school when you would organise a game among yourselves and everyone wanted to play out? The last person to be picked would always end up in goal because he was the worst player — and be blamed every time he missed the ball. Of course, I don't look at it that way. A good goalkeeper is vital to any side, so much so that many coaches and managers create a team by building from the back, making sure their team has satisfactory defensive capabilities before strengthening other areas. Keepers are always in no-win situations. Whereas outfield players make several mistakes during matches, which can go unnoticed or unpunished, the person wearing the number one shirt knows that every one of his is highlighted and could lead to a goal. In those situations we are the villains. We hardly ever become the heroes.

A keeper needs to be reliable and confident, possessing the ability to overcome any errors made and being doubly determined not to let in another goal, whether the one which has just been scored was his fault or not. People hate conceding goals, and more often than not they are powerless to prevent them. But even if you are beaten, you can draw a crumb of comfort if you have made it difficult for your opponent to find the net. It is important to remember, though, that a goalkeeper is part of a team, and so for every goal conceded it is the team which has been beaten rather than the individual. Instead of taking the view that it is one man against the world, goalkeepers should remember that effectively there are 10 players in front, who all want to get hold of that ball. Keeping goal requires dedication and concentration, and not everyone has the ability or the attitude to

play in such a position.

Anyone who knows me knows I don't mince my words, and while I admit that keeping the ball out of the net by whatever means outlines the basic job requirement of the most specialised role on the field, saying that goalkeeping is only about saving shots is the biggest load of nonsense I have ever heard. And rather than considering yourself to be the worst outfield player, you should look upon yourself as the best last line of defence.

Keepers should be the biggest thinkers in the game. They should always be asking themselves questions, analysing situations, as theirs is the most scrutinised position on the field and their margin of error is nil. For me, they should be mentally tough and determined to succeed. That's the way I am. There are two ways of approach — either you can say: "Okay, I want to make a living and this is a good way," or you can say: "Right, I want to win things and I want to be the best." In striving to be the best you have a chance of becoming it, and it shows a positive attitude which I believe is essential. Adopting the first line of thought highlights a lack of ambition and drive which makes getting up in the morning and coming to work a chore rather than a pleasure, which is what it should be. And you will find that the better prepared you are for matches, the more enjoyable you will find them. Train well and you feel great.

To be a goalkeeper you have to be an athlete, gymnast — you have to be able to bounce off the ground — weightlifter and basic footballer. Although you are the only player on the field able to handle the ball, skills with your feet for accurate, and sometimes powerful, distribution are necessary. That is especially so nowadays

Pat Jennings — one of the all-time greats

with FIFA's rule which stops keepers handling kicked backpasses, forcing them to clear with their feet. A goalkeeper also needs to be a bit of a psychologist. By that I mean training your mind on the play, trying to out-think your opponents and blotting out the noise — and abuse — from the sidelines. In other words, it's about being thick-skinned. Psychology is a major part of my game because apart from trying to be in the right frame of mind for a match, it helps me believe in my ability and to have the character to overcome any mistakes.

Goalkeepers have to analyse their game and, above all, be willing to learn. In football, especially goalkeeping, people must accept that there will be some skills at which they are not particularly good. Therefore, they have to work harder at them in training, and in matches a keeper should

try to force opponents into situations which allow them to produce their strongest skills. As you will read, I consider bravery to be something you are either born with or without, but most aspects of goalkeeping can be worked upon — even agility, which is also a gift given naturally. Look at the relevant exercises later in the book. You see, there is no point in being told how to improve if you don't take any notice. One thing I can't accept is people who are told what they are doing wrong, and never do anything about it. You *have* to be prepared to learn, no matter how frustrated you may feel. I've been in football for many years, I've played over 80 internationals for Wales and won Cups and Championships with Everton, but I'm still learning. I remember when I first started playing football I didn't have any vocation about becoming a goalkeeper.

I used to play in and out of goal as a lad. In fact, I don't see why anyone should have a yearning for a certain position when they are young. I think they should just enjoy the game. There is far too much pressure put on eight and ten-year-olds nowadays. You see children of that age wearing cycling shorts under their kit shorts, doing hamstring stretches and putting bandages on their knees just because it's what the professionals do. Then you have them developing groin strains! They have picked all that up from television, and then you have people coaching them and talking tactics from the sidelines during matches. I find that incredible. Why can't kids just express themselves and be allowed to have open minds?

THE EARLY DAYS

So how did I become a keeper? I never made a conscious decision about what I wanted to do. I think it was just a case of my being better in goal than out, although I went to one school where they wouldn't allow me to play in goal, so I had to go out. I played in and out of nets for my county team. One season it was me between the sticks, the next it was Eddie Niedzwiecki, who went on to play for Wrexham, Chelsea and Wales.

Playing out didn't do me any harm, because I got to learn other things about other positions. I think talent comes out as one gets older, and goalkeepers tend to be late developers. I just wanted to be a footballer — I wasn't bothered if it was in goal or not. I just loved the game. It's only when people pick you for a team in a certain position that you start to think seriously about whether that's your best. That's what happened to me. When I was 11, I was selected for my school's Under-14's, and I played in goal for a pub side on Sunday mornings when I was 14. I would say that the people who make a conscious decision and say: "Right, I'm going to be a goalkeeper now," never make it. While I desperately wanted to be a footballer, I never seriously thought it would happen because so many people fall by the wayside, so I got a job as a hod carrier. It was only when I moved to Winsford United, a non-league team, that I started to believe it was possible. Because of my job, I only saw the lads on match-days and it was a question of getting off a train, playing the game and going back home again. I gave myself two years there and luckily I had a good first one, which convinced me I could cope. I then started wondering what the next level would be like, whether I could play in the Football League. There were a lot of non-league players who could have, but they chose not to because of the money situation. I was earning more as a hod carrier than I was playing for Bury! Obviously the financial aspect had to be considered, but for me the main thing was getting a chance to play in the Football League, and Bury gave that to me in June, 1980. I didn't do that well there for the first two or three months, and it was then that I realised the importance of self-analysis, because there was no-one there for me to ask. Things improved and the following season — after just 39 League games, Howard Kendall signed me for Everton, where I alternated with Jim Arnold for the first team place before being loaned to Port Vale, where I played nine League games in the 1982/83 season.

The following season I had improved enough to play regularly for Everton and establish myself as the first choice keeper. Now I've made around 500 League appearances for them and have proved myself at international level. I am fortunate in that being a goalkeeper my top-class career can last longer than outfield players. The likes of Dino Zoff, Pat Jennings and Peter Shilton, who were all great keepers, were still playing at international level in their 40s, and providing I stay injury free and I still enjoy my football, I hope to be able to do the same!

This book is not the perfect goalkeeping coaching manual because, quite simply, there is no such thing. Using the experience and knowledge I have acquired during my career, it deals in some detail with all aspects of the position, featuring diagrams, exercises and photographs to help illustrate the points being made. It is aimed at players at every level — from the schoolboy or schoolgirl beginner (we should not forget the girls!, although for simplicity I have used only 'him' and 'his' in the text) — right up to the senior professional. Perhaps even some coaches will find it beneficial — who knows?

The book is designed to encourage and stimulate rather than frighten. After all, the best coach in the world is the game itself. I have to be honest and say that following my advice to the letter will not guarantee you a place in the full England, Wales, Scotland or any other side. I cannot profess to have all the answers — it's about what works for you. What I will say is that if you use this book as a guide, are willing to learn and show the right attitude, then you will improve. And that's a step nearer the perfection for which every keeper worth his salt is searching. Including me.

1

GOALKEEPING
THE RUDIMENTS

Becoming a professional footballer, especially in the top flight, is a common dream, but few people realise just how difficult it is to achieve. Without wishing to shatter anyone's illusions, it is important to be realistic about your chances of playing at the highest level of the game. It is for this reason that, for all your talent, determination and commitment, I would never advise anyone hoping to break into football to abandon everything else and concentrate wholly on that. In view of the success rate, it is too much of a gamble. Keep something in reserve, which means not neglecting your education. I know I sound like a teacher, and you could quite rightly make the point that I managed to make it to the top without an abundance of academic qualifications, but I have been lucky enough to be one of the exceptions to the rule.

Any kid, whose Mum and Dad believe he has something worth developing, will also believe he is good. After all, the chances are he will have gone through school and been one of his team's best players. But just because all three people are confident does not mean he has what it takes. Here's an example of two young keepers we've had at Everton. I won't mention their names because that would be grossly unfair, but to be honest I'd be more surprised to see them making it as goalkeepers than I would seeing Elvis Presley alive! I know it sounds harsh, but it's the truth. What will those lads have to fall back on? The day they went to college just happened to be the day when a highly-respected former international keeper used to come in to coach. But those lads never complained about missing his sessions — they realised that education is far more important than you can imagine in football. I never had any, and if I hadn't been a footballer I'd probably still be a hod carrier or a postman — because I like being outdoors. But I really wish I had had a better education. The thing was I didn't realise

that at the time. If someone had told me when I was younger to concentrate on my studies I would have told them where to go! And it is with that experience that I can say to people thinking what I did that they are making a mistake. Now, for instance, if my little girl brought a computer home I wouldn't know what to do with it. I couldn't help with her homework, and that disappoints me. Children are far more advanced now then they used to be, and they will have to be even more so in the future as they compete for fewer and fewer jobs. To give yourself a chance these days you must have a good education. As I've said, I got lucky.

MAKING THE GRADE

Assuming you are fortunate enough to make the grade, you should know that there is no such thing as the finished article. It's my firm belief that every player, whether they are at junior, non-league or international level, can always improve — if they want to. That includes me. Unfortunately people tend to settle for standards far lower than they are capable of achieving. My attitude is: if you're good at something, then why not try to be the best at it? Today, what jobs are there and what opportunities are there for your family? Surely it makes sense to go and do the best you can. It may mean staying an extra half hour to train or whatever, but so what? If you have the time, then it's important to use it, otherwise it's just a waste. Here's something that will make you laugh: I've got three Jane Fonda workout tapes at home! Why, you ask, does a big strapping lad like me need them? After all, they're not going to improve my handling or my kicking. But I look at them to see if there's anything I can learn to better my general fitness, my movement or balance. That's what aerobics is — and it's also what footballers need. In the past, teams have undergone ballet training for similar reasons.

This is all useful for movement, balance, spring and stretching, and you can still do your weight training on top of that. You can be big, strong, muscular and imposing, but all of that is virtually useless if you're not agile.

COACHING

Okay, lecture over. Let's go back to football. It is rare to have a coach with an open mind on goalkeeping. They tend not to allow the players to be individuals, and so often keepers are the fall-guys in the team, even though theirs is arguably the most important role on the field. Everyone seems to know the basics about goalkeeping—and get it wrong.

You hear coaches say that every ball inside the six-yard box should be the keeper's, but that's absolute rubbish. That's because most coaches are outfield players who have formed their own ideas about goalkeepers. If, for example, a keeper does well in a match, his coach won't study the way he played and consequently he won't be thinking about how he can improve further. This is particularly evident at schoolboy level.

Jimmy Gabriel coaches outfield players at Everton, where he is in charge of the reserve side. I could watch one of his sessions and I admit I wouldn't have a clue how to improve them. But I could watch a goalkeeper in training, see what he's doing wrong and I could have that out of him in six weeks. You will have gathered that I don't think an outfield coach should coach goalkeepers. Having said that, youngsters should listen to *everything* that is said to them; they should go away, think about it and even write it down. Then they should ask themselves: "Would that work for me?" You're not going to tell me that someone who is tall and not quick on their feet should follow a general rule and be in a certain position at a certain time, because that simply won't work.

That player should modify his game according to his build. I mean, if he's 18 stones he's not going to be particularly quick on the floor, so he's going to have to stand up even longer or go down earlier, depending on the shot or cross coming in. It's important to sift the good advice from the bad, which is why I've said there is no such thing as the perfect coaching manual.

GETTING THE RIGHT ADVICE

I'll give you an example. Most books similar to this give the impression that if you follow everything that is written you'll suddenly become world class. Sadly, it doesn't work that way. The pages of these books are glossy and colourful, and you'll find that most, if not all, photographs portray ideal, sunny conditions. However, because of our unpredictable climate and the fact that life just simply isn't like that, some of the general rules need to be broken depending on the circumstances. In Everton's game against Arsenal at Highbury in the 1992/93 season, their England striker, Ian Wright, cut into the box and let fly. The pitch was particularly heavy and the ball quite slippy. On a day when everything was perfect I would have thought about catching the shot because I knew I could get to the ball. But on this occasion, I didn't know how far I'd slide when I landed after diving, and I couldn't be sure that the greasy ball would remain in my grasp, so I chose to play safe and knock it away. The conditions are very important, and my advice to anyone would be to do what comes naturally first and worry about any follow-up effort if and when it comes. That's a far more positive way of keeping goal than trying to make a save look spectacular and brilliant.

Showing off is not my style and, besides, it can be risky. First and foremost a goalkeeper must prevent the ball from entering his net, and it doesn't matter how. A stop with an outstretched leg or even your backside can be at least equally important as a twisting, full-length save. The double save I made from Manchester United's Paul Scholes in the 1995 FA Cup final was raved about in some quarters—but not by me. It's not false modesty, and I'm not denying it wasn't an important piece of goalkeeping, but no way should it be suggested that it was one of the best stops of my career. I've made a lot better than that—not necessarily as spectacular—and no-one has said a thing. It's true you feel good when you've pulled off an impressive save, but I honestly wouldn't mind if I never had one to make. I did when I was younger, when I broke into the Everton side, because I wanted to show what I could do. Now, though, when I go out on that pitch, I want to do absolutely nothing. I don't ever want to dive. And the better my communication with my defenders—because they are there for me—the less work I should

have. If they can restrict their opponents' chances, then I'll have done my job. Of course, people will say I've had an easy game, but they'd be wrong because they won't have realised the work put in regarding tactics and general organisation. Those people should be saying that I marshalled my defenders well. You see, goalkeepers should organise their back line.

I hate people who don't talk on the field, either outfield players or keepers. Keepers who don't open their mouths give one of two things away to me: either they can't read the game—and a lot of them can't—or they're scared. Good communication is vital, and I'll expand on that later.

ALL KEEPERS GREAT AND SMALL

Goalkeepers come in all shapes and sizes, and that must be taken into consideration by coaches,

Gordon Banks — in action for Stoke against Spurs at White Hart Lane in 1970

the player himself and his teammates. Here I should point out that not everyone who wants to play in goal needs to be a giant. You will find that most small goalkeepers have tremendously quick feet and are exceptionally agile. Anyway, height isn't the most important thing. Timing is, as is the ability to take and make physical contact. If you have a good spring and you have good timing, then you don't need height to reach the ball. Most small keepers tend to stay on their line because they have a tall centre-back in front of them. You hear a lot of kids

being turned away by clubs just because they are "too small." I can't understand that. If you're small you can compensate for that in other ways. Okay, if clubs want to sign someone who is 6'4", then fine, and I accept that in England the game is being geared more and more to the high ball, which tests keepers. But you're not going to tell me that someone who is 6'4" is going to be good on the floor or quick covering ground. If your team has two big, slow centre-backs, then you need a keeper who is quick on his feet.

Gordon Banks wasn't the biggest goalkeeper

in the world was he? Yet he was the best! No-one turned round to him and said he was too small. Take Peter Bonetti. You'd think he was far too small to be a successful goalkeeper. But he had timing and he was exceptionally agile, so he didn't need to be that tall. Then there's Hans Segers. He's only 5'11", but he's an athlete and he's had a good career with both Nottingham Forest and Wimbledon since coming to England from Holland.

THE RIGHT TRAINING FOR YOU

Training should be adaptable to size and weight. If you watch anybody train, you'll even find top-class keepers doing what they like to do the most. If they like saving shots, they'll put on a session of shooting practise. I suppose that's human nature, doing the things we're good at. But that isn't really beneficial. What is, is doing the routines you *dislike*. If you hate doing work on your knees, like me, then it generally means you aren't good at it, but it's what you should concentrate on. If a keeper is tall, then he will be slow getting down to shots and so he should endeavour to improve in that area.

Before anything is done, I would advise coaches to start with the basics—and I *mean* the basics, such as seeing how their keeper catches the ball. Now there is a right way and a wrong way. The wrong way is to move the body backwards when holding a shot, rather than moving forward towards the ball. Kids do that so often because they are not balanced, and a lot of the time they fall over. To me, that's pure laziness. After all, I'm only talking about moving one step. It's basic bad habits like handling and stance which need to be corrected from the start.

But I'll say this: if, after being told of their faults two or three times, players still haven't learned, then they never will.

I will give advice to young goalkeepers, because I think they need it. But I don't like doing that to Jason Kearton, who is the reserve keeper at Everton. Jason is a young Australian with a lot of talent and who can develop into a top-class player. But I won't force any information on him. Sure, if I spot something then maybe I'll tell him. It's just that nobody ever told me what I was doing wrong—I had to find out myself. And I think that's one of the best ways of learning. It's got nothing at all to do with the fact that we are rivals. On the contrary. I don't want to tell him to be doing this or that because he's at the stage where I want him to do what comes naturally rather than filling his head with too much talk. I want Jason to do well, and if he takes my place at Everton, then great. I'd just have to go somewhere else.

LEARNING FROM YOUR MISTAKES

Don't laugh, but I think the best thing a goalkeeper can do when he goes on the field is be prepared to fail—because in a strange way that's being positive. You know that at some time you will make a mistake, so you must be ready for that— and be determined to learn from it. If, for example, a goalkeeper is at fault for just one goal during a sequence of 20 games where he has pulled off saves and seemingly played out of his skin, most people would forgive him for that lapse and say he's had a great run. But he knows that he will have made errors week in, week out, and it's just that no-one will have recognised them. You see, goalkeepers are their own greatest critics. You have to be ridiculously honest with yourself because if you're not, you'll get found out. You can't go round blaming everybody else, pretending something isn't your fault when everyone knows that it is. That's cheating, and it serves no purpose whatsoever. Kids do that a lot. They don't want to assume that extra responsibility or do that little bit extra which will take them a step further. That's what separates the good from the great.

Martin Hodge: a keeper who really worked at his game

NATURAL TALENT AND HARD WORK

If I didn't think players could improve on their natural talent, then I wouldn't be writing this book. One such example who immediately springs to mind is Martin Hodge, who made his name with Everton before moving to Sheffield Wednesday. I don't think Martin was the most naturally gifted keeper I've ever seen, but he put in hours and hours of extra training and that paid dividends. This was a guy who grafted to the point where he was close to getting called up by England.

Unfortunately, Martin had serious knee problems, but such was his desire and determination that he battled back from all that. It doesn't matter who you are, if you are enthusiastic enough then you will progress. There

are so many things you can do to improve goalkeeping from an early age. Hard work always brings rewards and I can't stress that enough.

I don't think coaches realise how specialist a position ours is. That's why I come in and work pre-season. What's the point in me running around a field? I don't do that in a game. I can tell you that my training is equally strenuous, if not more so. I could take Sebastian Coe and tire him out in half an hour doing my training. At most clubs, the keepers train with the outfield players and then they are given shooting practise from six yards. That's not good enough. Top clubs like Everton, for example, need a goalkeeping coach every day because without one, keepers hardly benefit from the training because the sessions aren't balanced. And I'd go so far as to say that if I were a coach, I'd tell my keepers to go to the gym and work with the gymnasts because it's important to develop a spring and know how to take a fall. Being able to land is a major part of being a goalkeeper, which comes under the category of bravery. For me, bravery is pure instinct — I don't think about it. I would say it is something you either have or haven't got.

Concentration, which I will touch on later, should not be underplayed, either. Again, that's where the psychology comes in. Keepers touch the ball intermittently, which makes concentration essential. There have been games where I've only touched the ball about twice, but I've come off the field dripping with sweat. It's really difficult focusing your attention on the other end of the field for 90 minutes. It's great for me when I play the likes of Wimbledon or Crystal Palace because the direct style of their game means I see a lot of the ball and that my mind is occupied. But there's a danger in being too tense. It's like if you read a book or study a small screen for an hour and a half. You start feeling drained. If you concentrate too much your mind goes numb, which can prove costly. Well, I never said it was easy!

2

EQUIPMENT

Mexico's Jorge Campos — and his kit!

GLOVES

Before a goalkeeper can go out and ply his trade, he needs to be kitted out, and there is more to his attire than merely a pair of boots and gloves. Not least because there are so many different types of gloves nowadays. It is unthinkable now for keepers to use their bare hands, but that was often so even in the 70s. However, they are arguably the most important pieces of equipment mainly because they provide good grip. Be warned, though; they are expensive. If you choose the most expensive, which sell at over £40, then I would say you are wasting both your time and your money. You would be better off buying two pairs for £20 because they will last you longer. It all depends on what you want, of course. Peter Shilton used to use gloves with a very thick palm, but I didn't like them. I prefer ones which are almost like a second skin, and I wear them dry as opposed to some keepers, who wet them first believing that will improve the grip. Most times I play with gloves which have a green palm, because I feel comfortable in them and the grip suits me. It's about personal preference, but you must try the gloves on before you buy them.

There are different textures of gloves, supposedly to suit the surface and the weather, but really you'll find they are to suit the type of ball used. Or more precisely, the coating on the ball. I try and find out which kind of ball we'll be playing with in our next match and in training I wear the gloves which best grip the coating. I've spoken to Chris Woods, the England and Sheffield Wednesday keeper, about this and he told me he uses three different sizes — eight and a half, nine and nine and a half — depending on the ball. I have a range of gloves which cover everything, but I realise that non-league goalkeepers and those at schoolboy or Sunday League level don't have that luxury. If I were in that situation and had to choose one pair of gloves, I'd go for those with a white palm because they haven't been dyed, and dyeing takes some of the grip away.

I use gloves manufactured by "Sondico," and to give you an idea of how they differ, I'll compare the "Southall Premier" with the "Southall League." The "Premier" has a special latex palm and is recommended at professional level on wet, dry and all-weather surfaces. This glove has a side entry vent, a special thumb cut out for extended strength, external finger gussets and vents for added comfort and better feel, plus shock-absorbing foam. The full-length extended palm offers an increased contact area, while the loop fastening wrist enables the wearer to have an exact fit. The "League" model uses three layers of different coloured latex on the palm to produce greater durability, plus a special waterproof membrane for improved comfort in wet conditions. As on the "Premier," there is also a side entry vent, but there is a full-length wrist with a triple lock velcro fastening. This particular glove is recommended for training and on wet, dry, all-weather and indoor surfaces. The fact that I have only spoken specifically about two models from one of several manufacturers illustrates the importance goalkeepers place on their hand-wear.

That said, you can be wearing the best and most expensive gloves in the world, but they won't be any help if you have the wrong technique.

Kids' gloves don't seem value for money to me because the footballs youngsters use aren't coated. Ideally, when a kid is choosing a pair, he should take the ball he uses down to the sports shop and test the gloves for the best grip, but of course that's not always possible. However, I have to say that I think youngsters may be better off playing in goal using their bare hands, although I am aware of the psychological advantage which wearing gloves can bring. Kids like to wear them not just for grip, but also for

Gloves — an essential part of the keeper's kit

protection against stinging shots. I'm sure most goalkeepers would agree that gloves are used to catch the ball rather than act as a cushion against stinging shots. But that's why youngsters wear them. That's why they wear tracksuit bottoms and padded tops. They think they are going to get hurt.

I always take spare pairs of gloves out with me when I play in case one gets damaged during the game, either as a result of a kick in the hand from an opponent, or the surface on which I'm playing. Most pitches in England have sand on them from September onwards and that can cut you. But again, I know that not everyone can afford more than one pair of decent gloves. In that case, I would keep the good pair for match use only, and buy a cheap pair for training. When I was at Winsford, I only had one pair

myself, and I used to train with any old things. My thinking was if I could catch a wet ball without gloves, imagine how well I'd do with them.

BOOTS

As a goalkeeper, you are going to use them far more for kicking than tackling, and these days keepers do more kicking than ever before. For that reason I like soft boots with a high back and which just cover my feet. Again, like a second skin. I wouldn't wear heavy boots — and, like gloves, there is a large choice on the market — because I feel they would restrict my spring. I'm 14st 7lbs, so there is no point in my carrying any extra weight. But, as with gloves, choosing boots is down to personal preference.

The main thing is to be comfortable in them. Once you have them, though, treat them well.

When I was at Winsford I always used to take my boots home, and I always used to sort out my kit the night before a game. Obviously at Everton that's done for me, but beforehand I had no choice, and I think that's good preparation. If you're playing non-league or at any level, you should treat your boots like gold because they can be so expensive. I used to put goose grease on mine to make sure they were nice and soft, and I would take out the laces and wash them. It may sound daft, but it's important to look after your kit. I used to put my undershirt, the small pair of socks I wear under my football socks, my shinpads and my gloves into the washing machine after a game. Sometimes I'd even throw my boots in as well—after taking the studs out. It may not seem the conventional method of cleaning, but it ensures you get all the sand and mud out of them. Obviously I wouldn't advocate doing that after every match,

but putting them in the washing machine once every six weeks does no harm. Providing, that is, you let them dry naturally and polish them well. How many people do you see pulling their boots out of a plastic bag before they play? That's not exactly professional, is it? You can't play in boots like that. And besides, if you haven't got pride in your footwear, then you're on a loser. I know the temptation is there to take short-cuts, especially if you've been having a bad time on the field. You start to think: "Why should I put all that preparation in if I go and make mistakes?" You wonder if it's worth it. But you have to show respect for the game—even if it does kick you in the teeth sometimes.

SHIRTS

Looking at some of the shirts which are on the market these days suggests goalkeepers are part of a fashion parade. There are so many psychedelic, multicoloured varieties, which are

'I don't take a glove bag out with me that often now—it gives the opposition something to aim at...'

expensive, but you should remember that while you may feel and look good in a designer-type shirt, it does not alter your ability as a keeper. Mexico's Jorge Campos certainly caught the eye with his dazzling shirts in the 1994 World Cup and he has become famous for them.

That's not exactly my style, though, and a few seasons ago I chose to wear black. Not as a gimmick, but because it made me look bigger and more imposing in goal and also because it was harder for opponents to pick out on a dark day. By wearing a bright top, the other team is instantly able to know where you are even in bad light. Peter Shilton used to wear all white in his Leicester City days, but players said he was easy to identify on the field. I figured, therefore, that wearing black should have the opposite effect. I don't go in for these fancy shirts anyway — although I was obliged to wear the striking yellow outfit in the 1995 FA Cup final because Everton were unveiling their new kit. To be frank, I would have worn plain green instead of black, but that became impossible when referees in the FA Carling Premiership began to wear green. Now, for contractual reasons, that yellow kit has to stay.

Sometimes I wear an undershirt — it depends how I feel. Usually it's one of the outfield shirts, but without any sleeves. This is because I don't like to be too heavy and because I like to be able to move my arms easily. As a parent, I would want my child to be protected as much as possible, so I would encourage kids to wear two shirts and maybe even a thermal vest.

CAPS

Another piece of equipment is the cap, although you see fewer keepers wearing them nowadays. I don't particularly like them because they make my head too hot, and therefore I feel uncomfortable. I agree that bright, boiling days are few and far between in our football season,

but on the rare occasion that one arises, some form of headgear is necessary to prevent being blinded by the sunlight, and I prefer a visor to a cap. In fact, I've had one specially made. It's tinted dark green, so I can see through it.

SOCKS

I wear two pairs of socks — a small pair underneath the long ones, just for added protection on the feet. But I don't like socks. I hate wearing them pulled up, as anyone who watches me play will know! I know it looks untidy if they are rolled down and that referees disapprove, but I feel more comfortable that way.

With socks come tie-ups. I don't wear any because I get cramp easily, which is the reason you nearly always see me with my socks rolled down! I don't like my socks being too tight. Anyway, I train with them rolled down, and I'm comfortable that way, so why shouldn't I go into a game like that?

SHINPADS

But I would *never* be without my shinpads. I think they are the most important things you can wear. Choose ones with ankle-straps built in because they give greater protection. Why train all week for a game and risk serious injury by playing without shinpads? They can stop you breaking your leg, and I can't stress their value highly enough. I wear them most of the time in training. To me it's just common sense. I mean, you wouldn't go out to bat in cricket without any pads, would you? It's the same thing. One thing you can be sure of in football is that you are going to have a physical challenge, so why not be as well prepared as possible? Hearing some people talk, you'd think there was something macho in playing without shinpads. I'm sorry to be blunt, but those people won't be saying that when they're in hospital,

Peter Shilton makes his point

having had 17 stitches put in their shins.

Another thing to remember is that a lot of non-league players don't have their own insurance, so if they are injured and are forced to miss work, they lose money. And they may have a family to feed. When I was a hod carrier, I was off for a week with broken ribs, but because I wasn't insured I had to go back to work as I needed the money. I had no choice. You try being a hod carrier with broken ribs!

PADDING

Padding seems to be the in-thing for keepers now, but I don't believe in it. Not for someone of my size, anyway. Most, if not all, other keepers wear shirts with padded elbows and shoulders, but I don't wear any. I've had it all taken out of my shirts. I just can't see the point of it. Protection? Perhaps, if the surface is frozen, but in that case you can always wear some padding. Otherwise, I think it's unnecessary. You see, I don't need padding on my elbows because I don't land there. Why? Because my technique is right. Sometimes I land on my shoulders, but

I still don't feel the need for any padding in that area, either. For me, padding is a gimmick; it's a way of selling shirts, as are the weird and not so wonderful colour schemes you now find.

However, I'm not against children wearing padding. In fact, I'd encourage it so that they can be protected while they are still learning and also because it acts as a confidence booster. It's sometimes thought that playing without padding toughens kids, but it doesn't. That said, the only part of a shirt I would pad for a youngster is the chest because that's where the ball often lands.

Many goalkeepers' shorts these days are padded, but at junior level they will probably have to be bought separately for the shorts provided with the team kit are generally identical to those worn by outfield players. If you have the money, then there is no harm in buying goalkeepers' shorts, but don't go overboard and get a pair of cycling shorts as well. These are being increasingly worn by professionals to protect against groin injuries, but for kids they are unnecessary. You see them wearing them only because the pros do. You also see children wearing knee bandages and complaining of hamstring strains for the same reason. Call me old fashioned if you want, but this sort of thing didn't happen a few years ago. Of course, speaking of protection, there's nothing wrong in investing in a jockstrap, for obvious reasons.

I wear undershorts when I train because there is so much sand on the pitch, but I don't believe in wearing tracksuit bottoms in matches. I can appreciate that some people do, and on hard pitches some keepers consider them necessary. It's just that I feel tired in bottoms, and they can weigh you down—especially in damp conditions. Even at Luton Town and Oldham Athletic in the days of plastic pitches, I'd coat my legs with petroleum jelly to prevent any burns before I'd consider wearing tracksuit bottoms, and I'd skid along the field a lot easier. If I'd worn bottoms I'd have stopped. When opponents see me just wearing shorts when their keeper is in bottoms, they think I'm mad. But that gives me an advantage, doesn't it? Because it shows I'm not worried about the conditions. I've seen some goalkeepers wearing them just because it's cold! There's got to be something wrong in that. It's different if you're protecting an injury, of course.

I noticed that Chelsea keeper, Dimitri Kharine, wore them in the 1992/93 season because of the cold. And he'd just come from Russia, where it's hardly a Mediterranean climate! Don't get me wrong: I don't see it as a sign of weakness to wear tracksuit bottoms, and I would advise kids to use them for training as extra protection. But not for matches, because I think they restrict your movement. Once again, though, it's about what works for you.

PROTECTING INJURIES

Another thing I do is tape a couple of my fingers over the knuckles for the simple reason that I've dislocated one finger twice. The tape just stops them popping out again. It does not restrict

their movement. Peter Shilton always used to tape his wrists because he believed they would be strengthened.

He was comfortable with that, and a lot of people copied him. But Peter was a big lad, who lifted loads of weights, which demands strong wrists, and I couldn't understand why he would need to tape them. The answer is because he felt better that way. It's true that you can sprain your wrist fairly easily playing football, but I differ from "Shilts" in that if I wore tape there I'd feel awkward. The less I wear, the easier it is for me to move around. However, I must admit I tape both my ankles to strengthen them, for the same reason as I tape my fingers: dislocation. It provides extra support for the ankle I haven't dislocated, and added protection for the one I have. In fact, I'm obliged to tape it and, to be honest, it feels sore if I don't. Taping is hardly geared to children's football, and I

Dimitri Kharine

think that the only time a youngster needs to tape his fingers, wrists or ankles is if that part of the body has been weakened by a previous injury. Otherwise there is no point.

ON THE PITCH

I don't take a glove bag out with me that often now. Apart from spare pairs of gloves, keepers put things such as caps, chewing gum, towels, sponges and tie-ups inside and throw it in the goal. Me, I will tie my visor and three pairs of gloves together, but I'll *never* put them in the goal, and I have what I believe is a good reason for this. Look at goals which are scored from corners for instance, and see how many times the ball enters the net on the side where the glove bag has been placed. You may not be aware of it, but you are giving opponents something to aim at. A striker can see the glove bag and can use it to pick his target. I've studied this closely. Perhaps it's coincidence; perhaps it's not. But it's better not to take chances, so now if I take a glove bag out with me I put it outside the goal. If players want to aim for it there, then that's fine by me!

I'm not a big fan of chewing gum. The likelihood is that you will take a knock during the game, and you don't want to find yourself suddenly choking on the stuff. If you want to stop your mouth becoming dry, then it makes more sense to put a bottle of water in your glove bag. That way you can have a drink, and so too can your teammates. I would also recommend keepers to put their rings in there as well. Take all of them off before you play because otherwise, if you injure a finger, your jewellery may have to be cut off. And if you're worried about leaving rings in your changing room, as most non-professionals are, then at least they will be safe in your glove bag.

Some players, including myself, coat their eyebrows with petroleum jelly before a game. I do it to prevent my eyes stinging when I sweat. I must have a lot of salt in my body, and so I want to stop the sweat dripping into my eyes and impairing my vision.

Ideally, if your budget can stretch to it—this is more important the higher up the scale—it's worth taking two sets of your kit to a match, especially if conditions are rainy and boggy. If you are weighed down by water and mud, you will be severely hampered in your movement, and so you will find a half-time change more than useful. Or even necessary.

My advice to parents is to choose the kit for their children at the best possible price. Don't be influenced by brand names or colour. It's important the kit feels comfortable—not too tight, nor too loose.

And remember: once you've got your kit, you *must* take good care of it. Not just the boots, but every item. Make sure it is clean for every game. It's a question of pride.

3

MATCH PREPARATION

To many clubs, it is of little importance how players train during the week as long as they perform well in games. I suppose no-one can criticise you if you spend four days in the bath, play a short five-a-side game on the Friday and go and score a couple of goals in the match the next day. In fact, it's not hard for professional players to be physically fit for games. Mentally, though, it's a different question—especially for goalkeepers. That's why you have to think positively, about the saves you're going to make. Naturally, I can't ignore the opposition, and so in the days leading up to the game I'll think about their players and how they play. That's something kids don't do. You'll be asking yourself how they can, when there is no Press or television coverage of their games and the names of their opposing players are unknown. That's true, but what I mean is that if a youngster has displayed a particular trick or shown he can strike the ball powerfully with his left foot, the chances are he will be looking to do that again the next time he's in possession. So why not take note of that?

What is good about youngsters is that they have an innocence and fewer inhibitions. They are so keen to show what they've got. There's nothing wrong with that, but there's nothing wrong, either, in pointing out where they went wrong or where they can improve, so that they can think about that as part of their preparation for their next match.

I stress that this kind of coaching must be done in a gentle manner and not rammed down their throats.

THE RIGHT APPROACH

It is so important to approach each game with the correct attitude. By that I mean going onto the field with determination and being prepared to work hard for 90 minutes. It's no good a keeper saying to himself: "Once I've made an early save I'll be settled for the rest of the game,"

because he may not even touch the ball! Goalkeeping is like any job: if you intend doing just enough to get by, it won't work because you'll find yourself snowed under. That's so hard to explain to children because the younger they are the less aware they are. When you're a kid, all you want to do is go out and play. It's only later in your football life that you start looking for ways to improve and you start asking advice. Goalkeepers, like any players, need people to talk to, and I think a lot of coaches misunderstand players. Sometimes just sitting down for 10 minutes with someone can be of greater benefit than playing for an hour and a half.

This may sound crazy, but I assure you it's not: check the length of your hair! After all, you have to be able to see the ball, don't you? And it would be tragic if, after working hard all week, you are beaten only because your hair went in your eyes and impeded your vision. It's only a minor detail, but it should not be ignored. I know, because it's happened to me! I'm not for one minute suggesting we should all go for the bald look. Just make sure your hair won't hamper you. Tie it back if it's too long.

PREPARING FOR THE MATCH

A good sleep is essential the night before a game, whether the kick-off time is morning, afternoon or evening. After all, if you're feeling tired or groggy you're not going to perform in peak condition, and you risk letting your teammates down as well as yourself. The fresher you are, the more alert you are, which means you will have sharper reactions in the game. That, in turn, means you will not only be better prepared to pull off a point-blank save, but also to read the play and the flight of the ball better. You should be bubbling the day before a match, but try to go to bed relaxed, looking forward to the game. If you're dreading it, then what are you doing playing? It's important you fill yourself full of positive thoughts on match-days—even if you didn't sleep well. Even if you're playing the top team, keep telling yourself you're going to do well. Keep believing you can make the difference. After all, you're a goalkeeper, and you can certainly influence a game. You'll be surprised at the effect this positive thinking can have. And if *you* look bright and confident, then imagine what that will do for your teammates.

Most professional games are afternoon kick-offs, and even though I have the opportunity of a lie-in on match-days, I like to get up fairly early. I expect I'm used to it, seeing as my body is tuned to training at 10.30am every day. I suppose, with most matches starting at 3pm, our bodies should be tuned into that time. It would definitely make more sense if we trained mid-afternoon instead of the morning—or play all the games before noon. But that's just me having a little moan. When playing for Wales, I arrive at the stadium at least two hours earlier than I would do for a club match. I just feel better that way. Sometimes, especially in Wales, the pitch is so heavy that we are unable to train on it beforehand, so I like to have a good look at it before kick-off.

Have some food before you play. Nothing heavy like steak and chips, but a light snack such as beans on toast, chicken and beans, scrambled eggs or pasta. When I was playing non-league football, I used to eat bacon sandwiches. Now I tend to eat ham on toast. Even though I never felt bloated, this type of food reduces the risk. But whatever you eat, give the food a few hours to digest.

WARMING UP

Once in the dressing room, depending on your preference or needs, a quick rub down or massage can be good to stretch the muscles before warming up. I realise, of course, that at junior and non-league level, such routines are not always possible—if at all. But that still shouldn't stop you from checking your kit before the game and putting yourself in the right frame of mind. Remember, though, that the bigger the match, the more the adrenaline will flow, and sometimes you can get carried away by your enthusiasm. That's why in big games, a lot of players become tired after half an hour—and that's why I gauge my warm-up on how I feel. If I'm playing Manchester United, for example, I know I'll only need 10 minutes because I'll be bubbling, ready to get at them. On other occasions, perhaps I haven't "got my eye in," so I may need longer to warm up.

CHECKING THE CONDITIONS

The weather and pitch conditions are also important. They are things I check when I go out for my warm-up. Look for where the sun is shining and which way the wind is blowing. Many, if not most, players prefer to play with the wind, but I don't. Sure, it can be advantageous and I can see why people want to capitalise in case it drops, but my belief is that if your team is playing against the wind in the first half, then it ensures everyone will be fighting and in the right frame of mind. And if you do play well and benefit from the wind in the second half, confidence is always high.

The sun, though, is a different proposition. It's a real nuisance. In the Premiership, however, most of the stadia are high, which is good because the stands block the sunshine. But if it bothers you, wear a visor. Rain is also problematic because it can make the surface slippy or sticky. In slippy conditions, you know the ball will suddenly skid off the turf and bounce quicker than when the weather is dry. This is especially difficult when the ball takes a bounce as you make your dive. As I mentioned earlier, don't just think about the initial shot or header, but also the

follow-up. On a boggy pitch the ball can slow down and make backpasses underhit. That's why I stand a yard or so further forward than I would do normally to take a backpass. On such a surface, you should expect mistakes to be made. I always pay careful attention to the state of the pitch. You may not be aware of this but the two goalmouths at Goodison Park are incredibly different. I become concerned if we don't defend the Gwladys Street end in the first half because the bounce there is so unpredictable, and with the area being cut up from 45 minutes of football, playing there in the second half is an absolute nightmare. The ball could just go anywhere, whereas the Stanley Park end of the stadium doesn't cut up as much. Another point to bear in mind is that these days goal-kicks can be taken from either side of the net, so choose the one where there is more grass. If necessary, make a divot with some sand or soil to ensure good contact with the ball.

Floodlights are not a luxury of junior football, but at professional and particularly non-league level, they can be hazardous to a goalkeeper. Such is the glare in certain non-league grounds that when the ball drops out of the sky it appears just as a black dot and is very difficult to see. It's worth throwing up a few balls before kick-off to see what effect, if any, the floodlights

have, rather than leaving things to chance when the match is under way.

Check all your kit before you go out. The weather conditions and the make of ball decide what gloves I'm going to use, and I try them out in the warm-up. One routine I run through is to get a teammate to hammer the ball straight at me from the penalty spot (*See photos 1–5*). I don't dive in this exercise; I just want to block each shot. I find this extremely useful for training my eyes to pick things up close to goal, as well as sharpening my reflexes. Sometimes the ball will be too quick for my hands and it will hit my face or my body, but it doesn't hurt. Try it. If you do find it hurts, then it should make you get your hands to the ball quicker, and that will do you no harm at all!

Don't think that a warm-up for a goalkeeper consists just of saving shots or taking crosses because that is not a true reflection of our duties. I've noticed at Everton that apart from Jason Kearton and myself, the other goalkeepers don't do any footwork in their warm-ups. I can't understand why that is because nowadays keepers use their feet more often than ever, so it makes sense to get used to kicking the ball as well as handling it. Don't forget, we need to have a good touch as well as the outfield players; we, too, need to strike the ball well. That's why

3

Warming-up
*1 Make the warm-up gentle
at first, beginning with an
underarm throw at the receiver's
chest between two keepers 6-8
yards apart.*
*2 Then progress to the overarm
throw from the same distance.*
*3 Balls should now be thrown at
the receiver's face with some
pace. On both exercises,
make 10-12 throws and
use alternate hands.*

I take shots during my warm-up. It's not to show off, nor is it purely for my amusement. There is a definite purpose to it. If I'm not striking the ball well in the warm-up, I know I have to concentrate especially hard during the game.

Normally I start my warm-up with Jason. We begin by throwing a ball to each other, just to get the feel of it. I'm fortunate in that I don't need to do any stretching, but, of course, there are many keepers who do. Stretching is best done in the dressing room before going onto the pitch, ensuring you are warm when you go outdoors, thus reducing the risk of pulling a muscle. That said, after a long journey on the day of a game, it is probably best to stretch after stepping off the coach to eliminate the stiffness of travelling. Stretch for as long as you want. It's all about how you feel.

How much of a warm-up is flat out? Well, that's up to you. As with stretching, it depends

4 A typical part of my warm-up. The ball is kicked between both keepers to improve their reflexes and handling. This is a great way of sharpening up before a match because it gets you used to the pace of the ball.

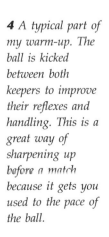

4

how I feel and also on the state of the pitch. I worked hard in the warm-up in a match at Crystal Palace a few seasons ago because the pitch was flat, heavy and muddy, so the ball could do anything. I did a lot of diving to get familiar with it, ensuring I didn't go down too early. You may say there is a danger of doing too much in the warm-up and tiring yourself out before the match — and you'd be right. That's why I said it's up to you how much work you do. When I'm happy I go off. It's as simple as that.

SUPERSTITIONS

Finally, superstitions. Nearly every player is superstitious — because if we believe some little quirk will bring us that vital piece of luck, then we'll go for it! Moreover, they keep us within our comfort zone; they make us feel good and confident, so psychologically they can be of value. Superstitions vary among players. Some go through exactly the same routine for every match, such as wearing the same clothes, putting the right boot on before the left or taking up a specific position in the line-up as we run onto the pitch. Of course, there are some who go nuts with their superstitions, to the extent that they take over their match preparations, which can have a negative effect. For me, it's about whatever makes you feel good and puts you in the right frame of mind to play. I mean, if you want to watch television, then go and do it. Personally, I couldn't do it, but I'm sure that would work for some people. All that said, I know I don't have to stress the point that you can't rely on superstitions to bring good results. It's down to you.

5 When catching ANY ball, it is important NOT to move backwards. You don't want to get into bad habits and risk falling with the ball over your line. For pre-match purposes, this routine can be done between the penalty spot and the goal-line. Distances can be varied in training, as can the number of shots made. Try 10-12.

4
SKILLS

BRAVERY

Put bluntly, if you haven't got bravery or courage, then forget it. It's a fundamental necessity for all goalkeepers because you have to dive in where it hurts. If that sort of thing bothers you, you are reducing your effectiveness by a large percentage, and it does not take opponents long to work you out. Fear is detectable, even from the slightest hesitation. There are some keepers in the FA Carling Premiership whom you may feel aren't brave, but I'd say that instead of their courage being questioned it's more a case of their being less determined than others. I've thought twice about coming for balls, but in the end I risk taking the knocks because I'm determined to protect my goal and I don't want to let myself or other people down.

DIVING

Quite apart from physical contact with opponents, there is physical contact with the ground. Goalkeepers often have to hurl themselves into the air to stop a shot or a header, and that means coming down to earth with a bump—literally! So how do you learn to take a fall? Well, for me it was always natural; I always came down on my shoulders which, admittedly, was not particularly good, and so I improved my technique. A lot of kids land on their elbows, but that's not something I'd recommend. Firstly, there's a chance of injuring that part of the body and secondly, the ball could bounce out of your grasp upon impact with the turf. That's why I smile when I see youngsters in goal wearing shirts with elbow pads. Applying the correct technique, they're not needed. Ideally, keepers should land on their side—the idea is to bring your hands in as you land so the ball can't escape. Practise this by diving on a painted goal-line and if you're doing it correctly you should see the imprint of the line down the side

of your kit.

Someone once asked me how to improve diving on his right side because, while he was strong on his left, he never felt confident when having to save shots to his right. My answer was to have someone throw balls to his right side, so he could get used to landing there, starting from a sitting position, then kneeling and then a squat, before moving on to a standing dive. If you have no fear about diving one way, this will be an advantage when faced with the dangerous situation of having to do so at someone's feet, which I'll discuss later. I like to judge people's technique when they are working from a sitting position. There are certain techniques of mine which are wrong, but I'm so used to them that they work for me. But it certainly doesn't mean they would work for David Seaman or Tim Flowers, and vice-versa.

ACCIDENTAL KNOCKS

People say you have to be mad to be a goalkeeper because you have to put your head and body in areas where others put their boots. But I don't go along with that. I would say that bravery is instinctive. In other words, if you have to think about these sort of situations, then you shouldn't bother trying to be a keeper. It's like a boxer in a ring. When he's punched, what does he do? He instinctively punches back. If he stopped and thought about things, he'd go and get hurt. It's the same for a goalkeeper. This is a job where you know you will be injured—and you know you will injure people as well. When you're young and you flatten someone accidentally in a challenge, you often feel a sense of guilt and remorse. That's something which happened to me, and it upset me so much it put me off the rest of my game. But that feeling disappears as you progress, and while no-one wants to see anyone injured, you find yourself taking the view that it was just one of those things, and that the same thing could happen to you. For example, I once punched my Everton teammate, Graham Stuart, in the face when he was playing for Chelsea. I didn't mean to, but I told myself that accidents like that are just part and parcel of the game. I know it sounds callous, but courage is comprised of aggression, although I stress that no way would I, nor any player, go out and deliberately injure an opponent. What I'm saying is that if you are prepared to take responsibility and go in where it hurts, then you have less chance of sustaining an injury. Or if you do suffer one, it will be less serious from a determined challenge than one which is half-hearted.

THE 50-50 BALL

On the subject of challenges, take the goals scored in the Premiership. Of those which arise from 50-50 situations between a forward and a keeper, see how many become 60-40 balls because one of the players decides he doesn't want to get hurt. I've seen a few goalkeepers back out of such situations. Should you suffer an injury but are able to continue, don't despair even if you feel handicapped by it. Remarkably I had one of my best games when I was injured, the reason being that in such circumstances you compensate for your physical problems with your mind. That's exactly what I did. I've played matches with broken ribs. In this instance I can remember hurting myself just two days before the game. I was fortunate enough to have a couple of injections beforehand which killed the pain. Naturally, not everyone who reads this book will be in a position to receive pain killing jabs, and so in that case they should not play. At the

A diving save against Arsenal in 1991

highest level, players will probably tell you that it is a long time since they last played without any kind of pain. Me, I'm always desperate to turn out even if I'm injured because I love the sport. I hate telling a manager I can't play. My view is that if I get injured, so what?

I've also played with injections in my back, stitches in my eye and stitches in my knee. You may wonder whether subconsciously those injuries would affect me. Perhaps they would others, but not me. In fact, the stitches in my eye woke me up. It was just as well because I was having a nightmare! Suddenly I got banged in the face and because I became conscious of the pain I went on to pull off two good saves! However, despite my desire to play, it goes without saying that if I didn't believe I could give a good account of myself, I'd miss out. Otherwise it would be unfair on myself, the manager, my teammates and the supporters.

I've already mentioned the way Wimbledon play, and I remember in one FA Cup tie against them at Selhurst Park in the 1992/93 season I wondered whether to go for a low cross, because I knew I would end up getting hurt. It was a dangerous ball in, so I had to go for it, and I got splattered as I knocked it away. Not a nice feeling, but an occupational hazard, you might say. As I've said, it's all about protecting that goal. Another occasion where I was injured was when Everton played Oxford United a few years ago. The ball was played across the goalmouth towards Billy Whitehurst, a big, burly no-nonsense striker, and not a person you would choose to tangle with. I knew he would score if I didn't make contact with the ball, and as I managed to do so he kicked me in the head! You see, a goalkeeper must be prepared to sustain injury, either from an accidental challenge or, in rare cases, a deliberate foul. It's a tough game. But there are a lot of times when I've expected to take a knock and it didn't happen.

RESPECT

Much of the time it's about intimidation and gaining respect. Generally, if you display bravery, teams treat you with more respect and become less effective. It's the opposite if opponents detect fear. Wimbledon, of course, have to do things differently. After I'd been kicked in the face that day, Vinny Jones, now a Wales teammate of mine, took a long throw-in and I remember him shouting: "Get on the keeper—we're bound to score now!" The cheek of that! Obviously Vinny didn't know me well enough then, because instead of intimidating me, that remark actually lifted me and made me more determined than ever not to be beaten. We ended up earning a goalless draw. Maybe he knows better now. Anyway, more of this in the next section.

It may come as something of a surprise to you that, unlike many others, I believe keepers are over-protected. Once an outfield player makes contact with a keeper, say on a high ball, the referee will generally blow for a foul in the goalkeeper's favour. But I don't necessarily agree with that. For me, unless a keeper has the ball in his hands, then an opponent is entitled to challenge for it. Of course, by that I don't believe players have the right to barge over or flatten the last line of defence. We have to be sensible about things, after all. More often than not—especially on the Continent—a keeper will be given the benefit of the doubt when challenging for a high ball. And while I don't particularly approve, as a keeper this can certainly be advantageous. For example, if the referee blows for a foul the first time you're in such a duel, then you're laughing because you know he'll always blow and so you'll be able to come for the ball confidently. But beware! Players know this, too, and they have developed other methods of distracting goalkeepers such as running across your back to block you. Referees tend not to look for that because their eyes are on the ball.

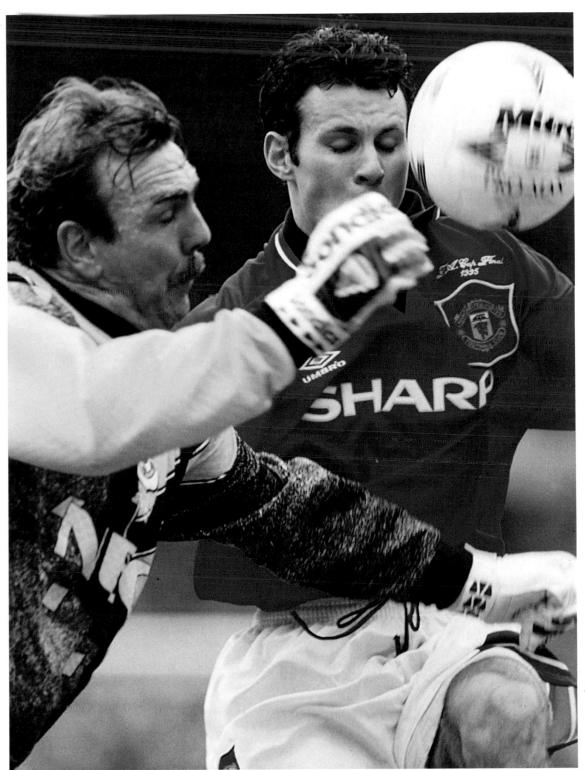

That's mine! Pulling no punches against Manchester United in the 1995 FA Cup Final

INTIMIDATION

I know goalkeepers can be intimidated in junior football—like the youngster who has made a save only for his opposing centre-forward to tell him: "Next time, I'll smash you!" Don't worry, I've experienced that—at that level and in the senior game. In an FA Cup tie against Wimbledon in the 1992/93 season, their big striker, John Fashanu, who wasn't exactly timid when it came to challenging a keeper, told me: "You come for the next one and it will be your last!" My response? I laughed. Okay, you'll say that's because I'm experienced, but in truth I've always been like that. I just used to think that was part of the game; that forwards would naturally test goalkeepers out, and as I got to know "Fash," I discovered that it was genuinely part of his game. What's more, he actually used to have a running commentary on the pitch with everyone he approached!

To be honest, the players to be concerned about aren't the ones who threaten you, but those who say nothing. Mick Harford, a lanky centre-forward who's had a good career with a number of clubs, never says anything, but he can splatter you! I've never bothered about people kicking me, although I have to admit it is a shock—especially the first time it happens. One such incident, when I was playing for Bangor City against Boston United, still sticks in my mind. But I'd rather not elaborate.

I shouldn't really say this, but what opponents tend to forget is that if they go out and hurt you, there's often a chance of revenge. You can be as sneaky as them. That's worth knowing, even if it isn't necessarily worth putting into practise. I don't mind the challenges if they are genuine and openly aggressive. Football is a contact sport and that sort of thing goes with the territory.

What I don't like are the ones who spit at you, who poke you and who stand on your toes. All this type of thing happens outside the referee's line of vision, but again it's something we all have to get used to, however unpleasant it may be.

If you go out on the field determined to enjoy yourself, it will have a relaxing, positive effect.

MOTIVATION AND TEMPERAMENT

The worst thing that can happen is to go out frightened. It's best to see everything as a challenge and gear yourself up to it. There's nothing wrong in being nervous—in fact, it's quite normal—but it should be an exciting kind of nervousness.

Use everything you can to motivate you, whether it's advice which has been given or just personal pride. There have been times when I've gone out for matches not feeling in the right frame of mind, but I've geared myself up to the occasion simply because I have a reputation to live up to. I have played in Cup finals, at home and in Europe, plus big domestic games for Everton, and I've also experienced vital World Cup and European Championship qualifiers for Wales. So it may surprise you to learn that the hardest matches for me are friendlies. In fact, I find them 10 times harder than other games. I hate them, and I feel I have much more to lose in those than in official matches. That's because it's harder for me to motivate myself when there are no prizes or points at stake. But I have to.

You see, a lack of motivation is often reflected in your performance, and teams take instant advantage, whether you happen to be a goalkeeper, defender, midfielder or striker. That's especially so at professional level. You just cannot afford to be flat when you're out on that pitch. And yet it happens. How many times have you heard managers say after a game: "They wanted to win it more than us"? Going back to that Cup game at Wimbledon, we knew how hard it was going to be so we were ready for it. The trouble was, we built ourselves up so much for it that in the next match, against Norwich City at

Goodison, we let ourselves go. Because Norwich's style and approach is totally different to Wimbledon's, because they play nice, neat football, we thought we didn't need to be as "wound up." A few of the lads were switched off. That was a crucial mistake, we lost 1-0, and it showed that it doesn't matter who you play, you should always have the same motivation. I try to approach a match against Norwich, or any other team, exactly the same as I would one against Manchester United.

Some players at junior or non-league level, for example, may find motivation hard after a long coach journey on match-day. They may be bored, just wanting to get the game over. That attitude is no use to anyone. Players like that will never be fired up for kick-off. Quite simply, if you don't want to play, then you should not have travelled. Try and relieve that boredom. I find listening to music better than reading when I'm travelling on the day of a game. Reading makes you tired, while having the radio on takes no effort, and you may just hear a record which gets your adrenaline pumping. It does happen, you know.

Motivation can be individual or collective, but you only have to look at Wimbledon — yes, them again! — to realise how important and effective it is. A lot of people sneer at this team, and laugh at them because they play their ghetto-blaster in the dressing room before kick-off. But that music really psyches their players up, and I doubt if you'll find a more motivated side. We now use a ghetto-blaster before Wales games. Okay, we may not be as good as Brazil, but once the music has boomed around the dressing room, we all believe we are. It creates a tremendous team spirit, and opponents certainly know they've been in a game when they've faced us.

If a match is on a Saturday, then I start my preparation on the Thursday before, and I would sometimes work on anything relevant to that match with Alan Hodgkinson, who took over Everton's goalkeeping coaching duties from Peter Bonetti and then Mark Harrison. You can use past experience as a source of motivation. For instance, when Everton played Sheffield Wednesday in February, 1993, I desperately wanted to do well against them because I'd made a mistake which cost us a goal when we'd faced each other at Goodison Park on the opening day of the season. Unfortunately, things didn't work out as planned because the referee sent me off for handling outside my area. But I used that experience as a means of inspiration before the next game against Wednesday. And I always will.

CROWD ABUSE

I've already spoken about the mental as well as physical strength required by goalkeepers, and the tough ones can even use crowd abuse to motivate themselves. What is designed to be unsettling can be turned into something positive. Remarks such as: "You useless fat ****" should be treated with contempt and fill you with the desire to prove yourself to the people making them. There was a Cup game I played with Everton at Bournemouth some years ago, not long after Wales had failed to obtain the desired result in a World Cup qualifier. The fans down there chanted at me: "You're not going to the World Cup!" But I went out and had a great game, determined that because of what they were singing, their team would go no further in the competition. I'm sure that those supporters had respect for me at the final whistle. I use that method a lot. Indeed, if the opposing crowd doesn't slaughter me when I take the field, then I'm not really happy. Something doesn't seem right. Yet I'm okay if fans who had applauded me before kick-off have a go when the game begins. I look upon it as a sign of respect. Obviously, the more experienced you are, the easier it is to overcome crowd antagonism. It's hard for a youngster if a few kids behind his goal keep telling him he's rubbish, but the only way to cope is by closing your mind. I just laugh at that kind of thing because there's certainly no point in worrying!

I think that when teams play at Goodison Park we should intimidate them more. We should make them feel uneasy about coming to one of the best stadia in Britain, but instead they seem to relish it. They have a good surface on which to play and they have good balls to use in the pre-match kick-in. We don't get that when we play at Wimbledon, while at Nottingham Forest, the visitors' dressing room is always roasting before a game which makes you feel tired. And that can affect your motivation. My view is we should do to others what they do to us.

It's one thing being motivated prior to a game, but it's quite another remaining so — especially if you have made a mistake. The mental side of goalkeeping is so different to that of outfield players and, as far as I'm concerned, they have no responsibilities by comparison. In other words, outfield players have far more opportunities to put right whatever they may have done wrong. If they make a mistake in the first minute, they have another 89 to redeem themselves, whereas keepers who have made an early error, can find themselves standing around like idiots for 89 minutes, completely powerless because they may not be called into serious action again. The hardest thing to learn is how to blot out the mistakes and be doubly determined not to make any more. This, though, is harder for kids to appreciate, because their view tends to be: "I hope the ball doesn't come near me again!"

Lots of things can affect your motivation — like conceding an early goal, or even just making a bad pass. But that's where you have to be strong. I confess I hardly ever listen to a manager in the dressing room. I tend to concentrate on getting myself mentally prepared and tuned in to the job in hand.

In any case, it's my belief that motivation from the dressing room for a particular fixture only lasts around 20 minutes, or maybe a bit longer if you're playing well. That's why the first quarter of an hour or so of each half against the "physical" teams like Wimbledon and Sheffield United is the most crucial part of a game. If you can match them during those periods, then you've got a great chance of winning.

PRIDE

What keeps me going during a game after those initial 20 minutes of each half is my pride and also the fact that I am playing for other people.

That should serve as enough motivation for any keeper, whatever his level. If I don't want to do the best I can in a game, what's the point of my being there? Naturally, there will be days when you have a nightmare — everybody has them — but you just have to be honest and accept that. But if you've given 100%, then criticism from yourself or others cannot be severe.

On the subject of dedication, what makes me mad more than anything else are the players who clench their fists and shout: "Come on! Come on!" in the tunnel. Because you know full well that once they get out on the pitch they won't say another word! Those people are the cowards; the ones who will duck tackles. For that reason, I just switch off when we go down the tunnel and just think about what I'm going to do. I would recommend the same to young keepers before they start a match. Don't worry about other people; just concentrate on your own game because it's not in the tunnel or in the dressing room where you have to perform — it's on the field.

Temperament can be allied to oneupmanship. For example, if we are doing well and we know the opposition is frustrated, then I'll try and take the mickey out of them. If a shot has come in and the referee has blown for offside,

I'll still try to fall over and save it, or if someone has had a shot I'll try to pat the ball down deliberately or catch it one-handed, just to infuriate them further. After all, there is nothing worse than being treated with contempt. Of course, I have to pick my moment, otherwise I'll end up looking a complete idiot. But out-psyching teams is important, even if you don't feel happy doing it this way.

CONCENTRATION

Earlier in the book, I mentioned the importance of concentration. This is harder for a keeper than for an outfield player, because generally he has fewer touches of the ball. It is in games where you have been rarely troubled that concentration can prove decisive, for you may have to make your first save in the dying minutes and you need to be mentally alert. Your legs and body may not have been sharpened in the match, but your mind must always have been, because the slightest lapse of concentration can lead to a fumble or misjudgement at the most unexpected moment.

Goalkeepers cannot win games; they can only save them. To win a game you have to score a goal, and keepers are hardly renowned for that, are they? That's why I've already touched on the dangers of over-concentration. Sometimes you see goalkeepers becoming agitated and really engrossed in proceedings when the action is taking place at the other end of the field! And then, when their opponents make a swift counter-attack, they suddenly find themselves beaten simply because they were too tense. I suppose the best example I can give of the perfect way to concentrate is when you're driving. How many times do you arrive at your destination wondering: "How did I get here?" It's as if you have been on automatic pilot. But you know that had there been any danger on the road, you would have been ready to react because, while

you may not have been aware of it, your mind had been focused on what was ahead. It's when you become impatient and try to overtake just for the sake of it that mistakes occur.

REFEREES

Finally, it's not just opponents and teammates who can test your temperament. There are also referees. Yes, those men in the middle can be infuriating at times, and they can certainly influence games. But you have to know how to handle them — especially if you're in goal. After all, nobody wants to lose their keeper, particularly for a trivial and unnecessary offence. To be honest, I've never had a problem with referees. That may seem strange coming from a man who's been sent off in recent seasons, but they were for technicalities. I find you can have a laugh with most refs at professional level. If they're all right with you, then you should be all right with them. If referees approach the job in the right way and are prepared to share a joke with players rather than be authoritarian all the time, then it is hard to see how there can be a problem with them. Because I tend to speak my mind, I've said some outrageous things to referees and got away with it purely because they have shown a human and humorous side to what is, admittedly, a difficult job. Players know from the first few incidents if a referee has that sense of humour. If he doesn't, then be on your guard.

One referee, Lester Shapter, used to check before every game if I was wearing a chain because he'd seen me wear one once. On one occasion he even ran the length of the pitch at Southampton to look! Mr. Shapter was a stickler for the ball to be kicked almost as soon as it's in the goalkeeper's possession. For example, if I caught a corner, he'd want me to boot the ball immediately even though we may have only had one, if any, players up front. All I would do then is kick into touch. I explained this problem

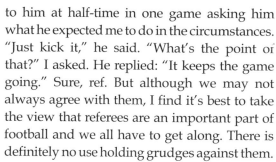

to him at half-time in one game asking him what he expected me to do in the circumstances. "Just kick it," he said. "What's the point of that?" I asked. He replied: "It keeps the game going." Sure, ref. But although we may not always agree with them, I find it's best to take the view that referees are an important part of football and we all have to get along. There is definitely no use holding grudges against them.

SHOT STOPPING

This is the essential skill. I think it's fair to say that if you can't stop a shot, then it's quite clear you will have difficulty being a goalkeeper! Having said that, I think the game is changing in that there are less and less shots to save these days—certainly in England. I feel a keeper's main concern now is with crosses simply because of the height of forwards—there are some giants around.

I've said already that the primary job is to keep the ball out of the goal, by whatever means. I stopped four shots with my face in the 1992/93 season. Not my most elegant saves, I admit,

but who cares? Nobody can say they were bad ones, even though they didn't do my face any favours! Some of the best saves keepers make look poor to many people. People associate the spectacular with the good, and that's not necessarily the case. I don't dive unless I really have to. Well, why should I? My game is based on saving energy; the economy of effort. Anyway, I can't really move until an opponent has hit the ball. Okay, when I see the angle of his body and I know the direction the ball is going, I can start heading that way. But what I hate seeing are kids—and occasionally professionals—bouncing on their feet on the lead-up to a shot or a cross. My reasoning is that when you're bouncing, your feet aren't in contact with the ground, and consequently you lose that vital split second you need for spring when you do have to dive.

For me, the style of stopping a shot is less important than it was, although there is a basic technique which I'll approach shortly. But, of course, applying that technique is not always possible. If I can't save or catch a ball, then I have to be able to knock it a fair distance. How many goals do you see where a keeper has got

Left to right: Shot Stopping 1 *The wrong way to stop a shot. I know some manuals approve of this method, not least the FA, but what happens if the ball takes a sudden deflection?* **2 3 & 4** *illlustrate the alternative method – scooping the ball off the ground, allowing the keeper greater spring in the event of a deflection.*

his hand to a shot or a header and the ball drops in front of him for an in rushing striker to tap in the net?

To me, that is truly disgraceful. Sure, you'll have people saying what a great first save it was and how unfortunate the keeper was with the rebound, but to me that's the biggest load of nonsense I could hear. Shot-stopping is not just about catching; it's about knocking the ball away out of the danger zone. Keepers should strengthen their fingers, to enable themselves to turn shots over the bar or around the post. And if they do, for some reason, only parry the ball in front of them, they should be quick enough on their feet to save the follow-up, otherwise they'll have conceded a bad goal.

And so to technique. Everyone thinks goalkeepers should stand in the same place every week for every shot and cross and do the same things. That's total rubbish. What happens if you're playing against someone who has a ridiculous left foot or some other amazing talent? You have to expect the unexpected all the time. In the late 80s Newcastle United had a most outrageous and unpredictable Brazilian striker,

Mirandinha, and he used to shoot from everywhere. When I played against him, I made sure I was concentrating all the time and not taking up any set position because, quite simply, anything could happen when he had the ball.

If you keep your head and body in line with the ball, then at least you have a chance of stopping it entering your net. The rest, on many occasions, is up to you. The correct footwork and legwork is also crucial on shot-stopping, concerning movement towards the ball and producing the necessary spring when diving. When preparing for a shot or header, have your feet spaced to provide comfortable balance and bend your knees slightly. Your shoulders should be bent forward slightly, with your arms down ready to expect anything. A more crouching style is best adopted if an opponent looks set to shoot from around the edge of the penalty area. This will get you well positioned to react to a ball struck low or at head height. Should you be required to move across goal before diving, don't cross your feet when you do so. It upsets your momentum and your balance, costing that precious split-second which can mean the difference between a save and a goal. The feet and the head should be the first parts of the body to move when faced with a shot or a header, the eyes following the flight of the ball *at all times*. The arms should be the last, being used to catch the ball or knock it away. Goalkeepers must always adopt a positive stance. That means being well balanced and ready to attack the ball rather than letting the ball attack them. Consequently, you should not fall backwards when collecting the ball as there is a danger of crossing the goal-line. Don't be so stiff and rigid that it restricts your movement and increases the chances of the ball ricocheting. Moreover, being rigid means a keeper is more likely to fall backwards when saving. But on the other hand, don't be so relaxed that your reactions suffer. Be strong enough to meet the shot but supple enough to

take the sting out of it.

LONG RANGE SHOTS

What points are there to consider on long-range shots? Firstly, you can generally tell when players will shoot from distance because most will have a big back-swing. Try and read how much time, space and distance they have so you can anticipate when they are going to let fly. Occasionally you can be caught out by an early shot if you read too much of the play. For example, if you see a player wide and unmarked, you may expect the ball to be passed there, but if the person in possession is crafty and fancies his chances, then a surprise pot at goal could be on the cards. Generally speaking, though, keepers should have enough time to anticipate a long range effort, and I can't say that's something I fear. Because

Close range action – FA Cup Final 1984

of that, it's widely considered that a goalkeeper shouldn't be beaten from distance. That's not always true. You can only do so much to protect your net, but if the ball is travelling at 90 miles an hour and flies towards the top corner, it's extremely hard to keep out. It doesn't happen that often, which is why those spectacular goals are remembered and replayed frequently on television. What's more, the further the distance, the more chance of the ball moving and playing tricks in the air. And different balls do different things. Don't forget, though, that in those situations keepers rely on their defenders to close opponents down and deny them that shooting opportunity. But I would say that if the ball travels within saving distance, keepers shouldn't be beaten from long range. I've seen a lot of goals scored where the ball has flown over the keeper's head. That's only because he's taken his eye off it. So be mentally alert.

An upright pose should be taken if an opponent seems set to fire from distance, the logic being that the ball will probably travel high, but should it dip or swerve, a keeper has more chance of reacting from an upright position than a crouched one. Almost always I stand on the edge of the six-yard box when anticipating such a shot. Well, it's going to have to be a real blaster to beat me and if my opponent tries a chip, at least I'll have room and time to move backwards. Unless it's a real dipper, that is, in which case I'd be powerless. Goalkeepers are only human, you know! On the subject of dippers, a bouncing ball is more likely to dip than one which is struck off the turf, so I prefer to stay on my line if a player is running to strike on the bounce. Dipping shots are not easy to keep out—especially for youngsters. On these, more than on any other, children playing in goal will dive too early and use little or no footwork. Instead of angling their body slightly so they can use their better arm to reach the ball, they dive straight back. Once the line of any shot has been read, the next step for a keeper is to reach the ball. That's where footwork comes in. It doesn't matter how tall you are, unless you move your feet you'll be in trouble. Lack of footwork can be attributed to laziness in most cases. You may only be able to take one or two steps before diving. That depends on your style, your ability and your vision, which can be particularly impaired on a shot from around 30 yards. The timing of your dive is also important, because a lot of people dive too early. But, as I said earlier, if you get your head and body in line with the ball you've got a chance of stopping it.

MEDIUM RANGE SHOTS

You have less time to see the ball when it's struck from medium range. From that distance, a player will attempt one of two things: either a bender or a blaster. If the ball is whacked and you manage to get a touch, you'll probably save it because the pace of the ball should guarantee a good deflection off your body. However, on a curled shot, goalkeepers need to put their own pace on the ball in order to knock it away.

Other things to be wary of on shots from around 18 yards are the risk of deflection and the bounce off the pitch, but the state of the surface should be taken into account during your preparation. For shots around the penalty area I would again advance to the six-yard box, and I would try to do so when the striker has his head down, so he can't see me move. I've seen a lot of children playing in goal who move when their opponent is about to shoot. That is wrong. Their position should be set before the shot comes in. It makes sense, because if you're moving when the ball is hit, then it's impossible to change that movement.

CLOSE RANGE SHOTS

Be cautious of the bouncing ball on close range shots, say from up to 12 yards. So many keepers, especially youngsters, are attracted to a bouncing ball, and I suppose it's a natural reaction to rush out to try and snatch it. But resist that temptation! If I saw a player running onto one from only a few yards out, I'd be standing on the goal-line. The only options he would have would be to strike the ball on the full or control it before deciding his next move. If I rushed out, I would give him another option of lobbing, because he would see the gap behind me. By staying on my line, the player could be tempted to bring the ball under control, which gives me precious time to advance and narrow the angle. I always try to stand up as long as I can, firstly because my opponent might miss-hit his shot and secondly because I want him to decide his next move, rather than have it mapped out for him. There are only a handful of talented players who can fool you in these situations, my former Everton teammate Peter Beardsley being one, but once you've seen them a few times on television you know their tricks. Obviously junior and non-league players don't have the benefit of seeing their opponents on TV, so their need to stand up on close range shots is even greater. This skill is also applicable to one-on-one situations, which is covered shortly.

POINT-BLANK SHOTS

Should you be faced with a ground shot from point-blank range, you'll nearly always have to rely on your legs to save. The secret on these occasions, as with one-on-one challenges with a forward, is to stay standing up and as big as possible—and I can't stress that enough. True, goalkeepers depend more on reflexes and instinct to save at point-blank range than anything else, but it's my belief that many players will lean back when hitting the ball, which means the ball will arrive at a height from the knees upwards. Bryan Gunn of Norwich City and Scotland is very good at making himself look big.

It's not easy, but it's essential. It's strange: the more you can keep still, the more you attract the ball. So don't fall backwards! I've noticed that's a major failing of youngsters today. I don't know if it's because they aren't as brave as they used to be or if they don't care enough. Stephen Reeves, who, until recently, was Everton's third choice keeper, is guilty of falling backwards, and it's something I've told him on many occasions. It's up to him to put it right.

By the way, if you do manage to block a point-blank range shot, don't let anyone say you were lucky! You've used your skill in staying upright and forcing the striker to make the next move, and you are entitled to be credited for that.

CATCHING AND PUNCHING

Not every ball needs to be caught. The type of shot or header, plus the conditions, govern your decision whether to catch it, punch it or parry it away. A ball travelling at speed can be sufficiently deflected off target by your fingertips or a flick of the wrist. The important thing to remember is to be certain and not take chances. Many Continental keepers tend to parry shots instead of catching them, and use their wrists to do so. While the ball will certainly take a good rebound off that part of the body, unless you beat the ball away from goal it is a dangerous way of thwarting an attack because you risk knocking the ball back in front of you. The palm of your hands provide both power and accuracy and should be used to push a shot or a header *away* from the danger area, not just to beat the ball out. Fingertips are useful for diverting the ball around the post or over the bar with greater accuracy than wrists, although they are not as powerful. I'm amazed how few keepers spend time strengthening their fingertips, considering they are as important a means of defence as their palms. I'm fortunate enough to have strong fingers, but a simple method of strengthening them is to do press-ups.

If you find it difficult or your fingers hurt, it's because they are not strong. Which is the whole purpose of this exercise, isn't it? Start off gently, doing as many or as few as your body will allow, and build up gradually.

If choosing to catch the ball, try to get both hands to it with your thumbs joining at the back to provide an extra barrier, which prevents it slipping through your grasp. While hands are a keeper's principal defence, they are certainly not the only means. Don't trust everything to your handling, and get your body behind the ball in order to have that additional protection should the ball squirm free from your grip. This is especially relevant on hard shots, where the pace can be too much for your hands, but if your chest is there as cover, that particular attempt on goal will be thwarted and it will be up to you to react quickly enough to save the rebound. The chest can come in handy when faced with a low shot or one that takes a wicked bounce. On shots or headers around waist height, try to hug the ball into your midriff to prevent any rebound. If you work on the premise that if the worst comes to the worst and you can't catch or even handle the ball, then make sure it hits *some* part of your body.

One of the most difficult shots to save is the low, well-struck one around the keeper's waist which forces him to dive. You have to be really smart to stop such a shot because all of your body — your legs, side and arms — have to get down in one movement. If the ball slips under your body and into the goal, it will be considered as a goalkeeping error, but making a save like that is not as simple as it appears. The cruel among you will no doubt remind me — not that

I need reminding — of the goal I conceded against Romania at Cardiff in a qualifying match for the 1994 World Cup when a long shot from Gheorghe Hagi slipped under my body.

Generally, though, I find placed shots rather than powerful ones harder to keep out because, as I mentioned earlier, if I do manage to touch the ball, its pace should be strong enough to deflect off target. I'd much prefer to see the strikers at Everton place their shots from inside the box instead of blasting them. I'm convinced if they did they'd score more goals. It's just a matter of composure. Allan Clarke, who played for Leeds United and England in the 1970s was great at that. So too was his brother, Wayne, who played for Everton in the mid-to-late 80s. He never gave opposing goalkeepers a chance. And, as a keeper, a chance is all you want. . . .

Generally speaking, efforts on goal which

Gheorghe Hagi

43

1

2

arrive at waist to head height are the easiest to save. Keepers should be comfortable with those. Personally, unless it is aimed for the top corner of the net, I prefer the ball to be hit higher than lower purely because I'm a six-footer and it's easier for me to get up than down.

ONE-ON-ONE SITUATIONS

Of course, it's not just shots or headers which pose problems — I'm referring to one of the most dangerous situations a keeper can face — a one-on-one confrontation with an opponent who has broken clear and takes you on. In such a situation, the most important skill for a keeper to learn is narrowing the angle. That is judging how far you can advance from your goal by the distance of your opponent, the idea being to give him as small a target as possible. The larger a figure you cut, the harder it is to be beaten. Staying on your line severely restricts your chances of saving a shot aimed for the corner of the net. It is important you take up your position before your opponent strikes the ball, in order to anticipate where he will aim. But this is not an easy skill because goalkeepers must take into account their own height.

For example, a tall keeper will be able to come out further than a small one because there is less chance of him being lobbed. Remember, though, that when faced by a player straight on, you will have to advance more than when faced by a player at an angle. Study the pictures carefully. On a one-on-one, if you come off your line too quickly you risk being chipped or lobbed by your opponent, which is something Crystal Palace's Republic of Ireland international, Ray Houghton, loves to do. These are difficult skills to master on a non-bouncing ball, which is why most players will try to dribble into the net when faced only by a keeper. Again, stand up for as long as possible when the player bears down on goal, in order to avoid making his mind up for him. The chances are he will be looking for you to commit yourself early — so don't! In a game against Liverpool in March, 1993, our striker, Stuart Barlow, found himself face to face with their goalkeeper, David James. James is a big lad and he approached the situation perfectly, staying up as late as possible and not making his move first. The result had the desired effect, unfortunately for us, as Stuart missed the target. This sort of thing is really a battle of wits, and the further you go in the sport the more

Left to right 1, 2 & 3
One on one situations are about decision-making as well as bravery. In this sequence, an attacker plays a one-two with his teammate and attempts to dribble the goalkeeper. The keeper must decide when to go for the ball. Note how he attacks it low, at an angle and with his hands, not his feet, despite the obvious risk of injury.

your reputation can help you if you're a keeper.

This is because—believe it or not—people try harder to score past an established keeper such as myself than they do against someone younger or less well-known. I know because I've experienced it. However, if a goalkeeper can use his reputation as a weapon, so too can forwards, but you must not let them. Don't be intimidated or over-awed when faced by a player who is known for being deadly in front of goal. Certainly they will feel confident, but you must, too. Concentrate more on winning the ball than on who is going to kick it.

When confronted by an attacker, it's important to stay cool, not to rush in, to stay balanced and keep low. The nearer you are to your opponent, the more obliged he is to take you on. Try and force him onto his weaker foot, and when the dribble does come, time your dive as well as possible and make yourself as long as possible. I stated earlier that if you're not brave, you're not going to be a goalkeeper. Courage is required when diving at someone's feet, as there's always the risk of injury. Ideally, you should make sure your head is behind your arms and shoulders, and that you attack the ball low at an angle. Keep your legs away from the ball. I don't pretend

that this is an easy save to make, but bear this in mind: the forward is always expected to score, so you have nothing to lose, and secondly there is far more pressure on him than on you. If achieved, this type of save can give you a great feeling of satisfaction and also a psychological advantage over your opponent.

I'm stating the obvious by saying that you have more chance of saving shots or headers if you face the play! But I feel I have to say that because you would be surprised at the number of keepers, particularly at junior level, who turn their back on the game. *Never* do that! Not even for a split second, for you risk being embarrassed by a freak shot or unexpected backpass which suddenly trickles past you into the net. Mind you, if you suffer such a humiliating experience once, I guarantee you won't let it happen again!

CROSSES

This is without doubt the hardest part of goalkeeping since there are so many variations of crosses. Because we're allowed to use our hands, people expect us to reach every ball played into the area, which, of course, is not possible. It's true we have an advantage, and

The perfect way to catch a cross. The keeper takes the ball at the highest point. Note how his eyes are firmly fixed on the ball and not on the players around him.

that can't be denied, but it's only an advantage if the ball is played in the air. If it's hit low, then, believe me, it's very difficult to get down. I'll tell you something: I love playing against teams who have a big centre-forward because I know what to expect. All they do is knock high crosses up to him, which is great for me as my hands will be the highest point on my body, whereas he is reliant on his head. Most teams, if they're clever, will try to play the ball away from the keeper to try and tempt him out. Crystal Palace and Leeds have done that to me, which shows they've been thinking, because over the years I've tended to do well against them. The fact that they altered their crosses pleases me because in a way they are paying me a tribute. Also,

those type of balls are played away from goal, which is always good for a keeper, and it means I have less work to do.

After shot-stopping, catching crosses is the most important discipline for a goalkeeper, and while you may be good at the first it certainly doesn't follow that you will be good at the second. A keeper who is weak on crosses stands out and he will always have a flaw in his game. After all, it's not much use pulling off three point-blank saves if you completely misjudge a flighted ball and it sails past you into the net. The catching of crosses can have a significant effect on a keeper's confidence. A good, solid take provides reassurance to both you and your teammates, whereas one which is fumbled or missed causes anxiety among your team, demoralises you and tells your opponents you are jittery. Whatever success you may have achieved earlier in the game is completely forgotten. If confidence breeds confidence, then imagine what a *lack* of confidence will do.

Because goalkeepers can use their hands, defenders look to them to rescue certain situations—especially if they are not strong in the air. That's why you cannot afford to be scared of crosses. Kids often are because they find themselves playing against people who are bigger and they are afraid of getting hurt when going for a ball. But that's something which often sorts itself out through experience. I've noticed at Everton that youngsters are easily intimidated when someone is jumping with them. In fact, I could just run towards a young keeper and I know he'd drop the ball. But, as I say, that problem can be solved. You have to be prepared to be jostled when going for a high ball—even by players whose sole intention is to distract and annoy you, not to win the ball. The main thing is not to be intimidated. Just maintain your concentration and think positively. You still have an advantage over them because you can use your hands.

The **WRONG** *way to punch! Here, the ball just drops pathetically off the fist because the keeper's timing was wrong. These exercises are best practised with a server lobbing the ball over the bar from a position behind the goal.*

The basic technique in collecting crosses is to take the ball at the highest point, before it drops. That often requires the arms to be outstretched and the feet off the ground. Waiting for the ball to drop is dangerous because it offers opponents the opportunity to nip in and win the race for possession. In such situations, a keeper's handling advantage is lost, usually as a result of laziness or poor judgement. As with shots, get your head and body in line with the flight of the ball when possible and keep your eyes on the ball at all times as that flight can vary because of pace, swerve, spin, wind and deflections. Remember to be positive.

Any hesitation or sudden change of mind seriously affects your chances of making a proper take, which doesn't really put your teammates in a favourable position. Decide your move as quickly as possible after the ball has been kicked. By all means anticipate where the ball will go, but don't go racing out. What you must not do, either, is flap, palm or try to fingertip the ball away. That's simply not good enough. It's very risky because you don't get any distance and

it tells your opponents you are jittery, and you can bet your life they'll be hoisting the ball high again. Palming is fine, however, if the ball is dropping around the crossbar, providing you push it over for a corner and do not take any chances.

By the way, don't forget your footwork. Good footwork will ensure you are balanced correctly and able to make an effective take-off, which is best done on one leg, height being maximised by the use of your arms to lever you up. Remember, the ball won't necessarily come to you. It's more a matter of you going to claim it—and you must let your defenders know when you do. This is where good communication comes in. Shout to your teammates that it's going to be your ball. By doing that you reduce the risk of bumping into your own players or have you and them needlessly contending for the ball. Of course, should you choose to stay on your line, then you must also shout to your defenders to clear so they know exactly what you are doing. When you do come to collect, if the ball is caught at its highest point, its pace

The **RIGHT** way to punch. The keeper gets greater height on take-off and he attacks the ball, punching through it one-handed.

The technique is similar with a two-fisted punch. Again, the keeper attacks the ball and punches it high to gain both distance and time.
Try this until you feel confident and until progress has been made.

can pull your arms backwards as if they are coming out of their sockets. Don't worry about this because I assure you they won't! Once the ball is in your grasp, try to bring it down and hug it in to your body for extra security.

Don't for one moment think that if you are small you are severely handicapped when it comes to crosses. Yes, the taller you are the greater advantage you should have, but as I said early on in the book, what tall keepers gain in inches, they tend to lack in footwork or agility. They are not able to move across goal as quickly as smaller keepers. If you aren't tall, it's important you develop a good spring off the ground which, if achieved, reduces your height disadvantage. Goalkeepers, whatever their size, *can* improve their technique on crossing; unlike bravery, it's not something you've either got or haven't got. I remember playing for Bury reserves against Leeds reserves, and before the match the boss, Wilf McGuinness, told me that he wanted me to try and get every ball in the area. He wasn't bothered if I missed the occasional cross and he obviously knew the risks in making me come for everything, but having the backing of the manager gave me the confidence to come off my line. Finding myself punching the ball at the edge of the penalty box increased that confidence, as it showed that I did have the ability to be positive. Wilf had given me license to command my area and he was willing to shoulder the responsibility for anything that went wrong. But what he was concerned about was whether I would learn from this exercise — and I did. So many keepers are tied to their line simply due to the fear of risking coming for a cross. You can't say that about Bruce Grobbelaar, who had a marvellous career with Liverpool. He had no fears about coming for anything, and yet people still criticised him for that. That's something I can't understand. For every two or three centres that Bruce has dropped or missed, he's safely collected two or three hundred. But unfortunately

no-one remembers them.

Just as not every shot or header *needs* to be caught, the same applies on crosses.

PUNCHING

Punching is both a useful and effective alternative, particularly if a keeper's path to the ball is impeded. Small keepers probably punch more often than tall ones, and while it is often regarded as a desperate measure, don't underestimate its value. Clearing the penalty area and its immediate vicinity with a punch not only buys your team time, it also gives it a chance of regaining possession, depending on where the ball falls. Obviously, catching is a far safer option, but it is much better to punch a cross than to attempt to gather one cleanly amid a host of bodies. If you punch safely you won't be criticised, but if you mess up or drop a catch. . . .

Punching may be effective, but that doesn't mean it is easy. In fact, it is quite tricky to master, both the one-fisted and two-fisted type. Basically, a one-fisted punch — used mainly on balls coming in from the flanks — is a jabbing action, where your arm need only move a short distance and what matters is making good contact with the ball. The actual punch should be straight and high in order to gain distance and time. Take-off is better on one leg, but this is not always possible if you find yourself among a crowd of players. The principles for the two-fisted punch are similar. This type of clearance is mainly employed when the ball is played straight at a goalkeeper, and more power can be generated this way than with just one fist. Once again, it's best to punch high and far. Study the photographs on pages 48 and 49.

THE NEAR POST

One area of the goal which requires as much protection on crosses as on shots is the near post. Keepers can be made to look stupid if they are beaten at the near post and they leave themselves open to all sorts of criticism. No-one wants to concede a goal there, but unfortunately it happens. I've suffered that painful experience, notably against Liverpool at Anfield in August, 1991, when my Wales teammate, Dean Saunders, fired between me and my left post at the Kop end in a game Everton lost 3-1. I was absolutely slaughtered afterwards for letting in such a goal, yet the shot was struck from close range and at great speed.

The reason why the near post should be covered is to cut down the scoring or crossing options of your opponent. By attempting to take the ball early there you can thwart in-rushing strikers, so your positioning is important. If a centre is played in towards the near post, then I want to be right against it because that way I only have one way to move. Not every keeper agrees with that theory, believing that if they stand away from the post they create a bigger target. I just feel that you don't need to create a bigger target in that position and that surely the fewer choices of movement you give yourself, the better. A classic example of a keeper "showing" the near post is Liverpool's goal in the 1971 FA Cup final. Arsenal's Bob Wilson was expecting Steve Heighway to cross from the left, but by leaving his line he also left his near post exposed, allowing Heighway to score and embarrass him. Cue the criticism.

Because a goalkeeper's position is crucial when it comes to coping with crosses, I believe he should know where he is standing in the goalmouth. By saying I like to stand next to the near post for balls played towards there, it's only logical that the best position to take up for deeper crosses is at the far post. It is much easier to run forwards than backwards, so should the ball be held up by a deflection or the wind and fly short, you'll be able to run towards it in a forward direction. You will find your positional sense improves with experience.

SWEEPING

As a result of the rule which forbids goalkeepers to handle kicked backpasses, sweeping has taken on a greater importance. But how much so depends on the team you play for and the team you play against. Put simply, if the defence drops deep, then a keeper can't sweep. If you're in a team which plays a flat back-four and which pushes up, then probably the best place to stand for safety is on the penalty spot. Really, though, it depends on where the ball is. For example, if your defence is up to the halfway line, you should stand further forward and not give the other team 70-yards or so in which to play the ball. In that situation, the further out from goal you are the better your chances of reaching the ball. I tend to look at the players and where they are likely to run rather than the ball, so I can anticipate a pass and hopefully win the race for possession.

Goalkeepers now have to be more all-round players and they can be more cruelly punished on any errors, and I don't just mean by goals. As I know to my cost, a handball out of the area or a mistimed tackle can lead to a sending off, which I think is scandalous. That said, at the risk of annoying the purists, I admit I would consider bringing down an opponent because all I'm concerned about is protecting my goal.

I haven't found I've needed to alter my standing position following the rule change, because the Everton defence hasn't changed it's way of playing. However, some sides, like Sheffield United, force their keeper to stand further forward, as their back-four sprints out as soon as he touches the ball.

I've said that keepers need to have better ball skills than before, but they shouldn't be expected to turn into a Pele. When faced with a sweeping situation, you should always ask yourself whether it's best to clear the ball or play it to a teammate. It's important to remember, however, that we are goalkeepers and our main skill is with our hands, not our feet. So it's for that reason that I tend to whack the ball upfield for safety. I would advise you to do the same, and not take chances. Unless you have loads of time to find a teammate, there is absolutely no need to try and be clever, no matter how good you are as an outfield player.

Because you can look ridiculous if things go wrong.

Colombia's eccentric keeper Rene Higuita has never been afraid of sweeping. The trouble was, however, he fancied himself as an outfield player and rather than do the simple thing, he would try to dribble opponents well outside his area. Not surprisingly, he occasionally lost possession, notably against Cameroon in the second round of the 1990 World Cup, which resulted in a goal and elimination from the tournament.

So what do you do if you're running straight and are on a collision course with an attacker? First, what not to do is boot the ball straight, for you risk striking your opponent and seeing the rebound end up in your net. Try and angle your approach slightly differently so you wouldn't be clearing directly against him, and why not attempt a clearance with your weaker foot rather than turning your body to enable you to kick with your stronger one? It's worth practising this in training, just in case you are forced into this type of situation. Don't be afraid to take what you've worked on in training into a game. After all, that's the only way you will improve, isn't it?

DISTRIBUTION

The method of distribution depends on the style of your team. If you are fortunate to play in one which has defenders of the quality of former Liverpool players Alan Hansen or Mark Lawrenson, for example, then you're better off giving the ball to them because they are good enough to build attacks from the back. But if your style is that of Wimbledon, then there is no point in playing through your defence, as your strong point is launching balls forward.

Distribution is a skill often underestimated and neglected by goalkeepers, but its importance

Rene Higuita losing out to Cameroon's Roger Milla, Columbia v Cameroon, Italia '90

must be stressed. After all, there is little point in pulling off a superb save if all you do is return possession to your opponents with a poor clearance. Apart from halting attacks, keepers can start them with a quick throw or an accurate kick. Indeed, such is the evolution of football that they are even called upon to pressurise rival defences by coming out of their area to boot the ball long while their own rearguard has moved upfield. Of course, if your forwards aren't up to standard, it can be soul destroying for a goalkeeper to kick the ball because it will probably come straight back.

Sometimes opponents' tactics dictate your form of distribution. If, when you have the ball in your hands, the other team squeezes up and puts pressure on your defenders, then you have no option but to clear upfield, preferably with someone to aim for. Personally, I like it when Everton play with a target man, like Paul Rideout or Duncan Ferguson — they stand out as people I can find. If they are not playing, then I generally try to pick out one of our wide men rather than make a hit and hope clearance which could fall anywhere. It's only when we're lacking such figures that I go for distance, aiming for the corners of the pitch.

Opposite page & left: The overarm throw

53

The underarm throw

THROWING

Throwing is the most accurate form of distribution, and, believe it or not, it's the one I most favour. I know how much criticism I get for not throwing the ball out often, but unfortunately nowadays there aren't too many defenders comfortable in possession. Certainly that's the case in Britain. When you do throw, you need to make sure your grip on the ball is firm, especially when you are about to release it. But beware of the wind! This is something you must take into account during your preparation. A good way of testing the strength of the wind is to see how far you can kick and throw the ball from both ends of the field. That way you can know your distances and which form of distribution is necessary. An overarm, underarm or even two-handed throw can start an attack quickly, although the last two would mainly be used when teammates are close by. When you are in possession, always look to see if a quick throw out is possible, and whether the receiver has time and space in which to manoeuvre. Once again, though, you must know your players.

For example, it's risky throwing the ball to someone around the box who doesn't have good control. The chances are they don't want the ball anyway. Bear in mind that the lower your pass the easier it is to control. The photographs on pages 52-53 illustrate the technique.

In the underarm throw the technique is similar, with the keeper bending while leaning backwards and extending his throwing arm. Note how the standing leg is bent. Then, as with the overarm throw, the keeper thrusts his body forward to release the ball, following the motion through.

KICKING

In Britain, most keepers choose to kick the ball, but those kicks must be adaptable to the wind. The drop-kick, for example, is frequently used when it is windy because the ball travels low and consequently it travels further. It is also a fairly accurate method of picking out players, although it is one to be wary of when conditions are boggy because the ball can either stick or bounce badly in the mud, resulting in a miss-hit which could present teams with an unexpected

The Drop-kick

The volley: keep your eyes on the ball as it is dropped from waist height, and strike it before it reaches the ground. As with the drop-kick, the movement should be smooth and comfortable. Practise each session for height and distance until you feel there is improvement.

scoring opportunity. This is the correct way to drop-kick: release the ball at waist height and strike it just after it bounces up off the ground. Keep your eyes fixed on the ball. Practise each session for accuracy until you feel there is an improvement.

If it's distance you require, then clear on the volley. This is not as accurate a means of distribution as the throw or drop-kick, but it is the most common one and probably the safest. Naturally, the younger you are the less able you will be to pick out players, so distance is important for players at junior level. Pat Jennings, the great Northern Ireland keeper, always went for distance. His theory was a long kick to the edge of the opposing penalty area would create far more pressure than a short, accurate one to the halfway line. He has a point. Indeed, Pat actually *scored* from long clearances!

GOAL-KICKS

Goal-kicks, if they are not played short around the box to start an attack, are hit long. This is not an easy technique, especially for youngsters,

but it can certainly be improved as the drills show. As with all clearances from hands, keep your head down and your eyes on the ball, and follow through when you have kicked. A good swing is important and this can be developed by trying it slowly in practise at first and then speeding it up. Practise won't necessarily make you perfect, but it will certainly improve your technique.

I mentioned when talking about sweeping that it is best to adopt a safety first policy when having to kick a moving ball. Having said that, I've not always practised what I preach. In one game for Wales, I chipped a ball to a teammate

Close-up photograph showing how and where the ball should be struck when taking a goal-kick.

The goal-kick: *see how the keeper's head is down, his eyes are on the ball, and his standing foot is alongside the ball when he makes contact. Remember to kick through the ball and to follow through as if you were playing a golf shot. As with the other kicking exercises, practise this until you have improved in distance and accuracy.*

over an opponent's head. It was a stupid thing to do, really, but I just felt confident at the time. My advice, though, is go for safety when dealing with a kicked backpass unless you have time to find a teammate. That means aiming for touch or distance. Safety first also applies when dealing with a clearance or interception which may be construed as a backpass by certain referees. In these circumstances some referees will tell you if you can pick the ball up, but not all will. Therefore it's best not to take chances, so you should clear with your feet.

Always look before you distribute, whatever your method. It's no good my just catching the ball if I don't do anything with it. I always go out with the attitude of looking for things, rather than just hoping things will happen. If you look for things, you're being positive, and if you're being positive things will happen for you. If you let the game dictate to you, you will be in trouble. Of course, circumstances—and not just the weather—can dictate what form of distribution should be taken, and how quickly. It could be that the referee is someone who insists the ball is cleared as soon as it reaches

the goalkeeper. In that situation, and if your side plays with only one person up front, it is best to kick the ball down the touchline. That way it is more beneficial to concede a throw-in than hand back possession in open play, for the chances are your lone striker would lose out to his two markers. Another aspect to consider is fatigue. If your back-four has been overrun for long periods, then assuming your team is not chasing the game, my advice would be to take time releasing the ball to give your colleagues a breather. Supporters—and some strikers—prefer a quick distribution in such circumstances, but they don't appreciate your position. Remember, you can visualise better than anyone on the field, so *you* decide what to do.

One thing which can hamper a speedy clearance—and I'm talking from experience—is the colour of the seats in the stadium. Think I'm crazy, do you? Well, consider this. Your team plays in blue and you're trying to pick out a run from midfield or wherever, but suddenly you lose your man because he's been camouflaged by the blue seats in the background. I know this problem only arises at top-level, but you'd be surprised how frequently it happens. It's something which particularly annoys me. As you may have guessed!

COMMUNICATION

Communication in every area of the field is vital, but it is especially so between a goalkeeper and his defence. You have to make your defence aware of where opponents are. The information you give must be clear, precise and short, and it consists of tactical awareness, praise and criticism. If a player needs marking, has been given too much room or is making a run, then it's up to you to tell your defenders. If one of your teammates has made a timely tackle or interception, don't be reluctant to pat him on the back and tell him he's done well. Appreciation serves as the best confidence booster. Equally, though, if a player has failed to obey your call or has left an opponent unmarked, then you have every right to have a go, to ensure there will be no repetition of the error.

A goalkeeper should work in tandem with his defence, informing it of the positions of opponents, both for marking purposes and for the use of the offside trap. Remember that a keeper is like an extra pair of eyes and the defence is something you have to control and organise; for example, making sure it sets an offside trap by moving forward in line when the ball has been cleared up the field. Note, too, that it's you who has to decide whether to collect a ball played between you and the last line of defence. If it's yours, claim it with a positive shout. If it's not, then tell your teammates to clear. A quick, clear call restricts the chances of misunderstanding which could be costly. It is vitally important you know each other's movements and positioning. For example, if a teammate is in possession and has an opponent closing in, then let him know because they may

not be aware. Equally, you should inform them if they have time and space when they are on the ball.

LEADERSHIP

It can be argued that goalkeepers should make the ideal captains since they can see all the way down the field and they should be good organisers. I have captained both Everton and Wales and I haven't found it a problem. Actually, provided a keeper is vocal, I can't see anything wrong. Yes, I can see the other end of the field, and yes, I believe I can still influence my teammates from where I stand. Nothing anyone says will convince me otherwise.

I think defenders find it comforting to have a goalkeeper who shouts and organises, and who lets you know he is there. Don't think that a keeper who shouts and bawls throughout a game is a big-head, because that is not necessarily true. It may be annoying and not always needed, but of the two extremes it's far better to have a keeper who constantly shouts than one who is permanently silent because it shows you are alert. What's more, it shows you are not frightened. But it's all about knowing your players, because they are all different. For instance, Martin Keown, who left Everton for Arsenal in 1993, was someone you had to encourage all the time, otherwise it was no use telling him anything. On the other hand, you can say something sensible to Matt Jackson and he'll take it in. My skipper at Everton, Dave Watson, is different class because he will respond to what you tell him. But communication is not solely about shouting and bawling. If you can get some banter going among your teammates, then it will help to lift spirits. You have to remember that football is a team game and so I hate walking into a quiet dressing room. Surely, if no-one is talking and there is no noise, there must be something wrong.

*Sorting out
the back four*

I touched on concentration earlier in the book, and rather than make that a separate category, I class it under communication. There is nothing worse than not touching the ball for 20 minutes and then suddenly being expected to be razor sharp. But razor sharp is what you have to be, which is why I like to shout regularly at the players around me. It keeps me aware of what is happening even though I may not have been actively involved for some time. This is mutually beneficial, for it tells my defenders that I'm still alive and it ensures they keep on their toes. Being objective, I'd say that is one of Jason Kearton's faults. He's too quiet. I've spoken to him about this, and I'm glad to say he's definitely improving. I even told him once that someone from Chelsea came to watch him but they decided against following up their interest because he was far too quiet. Jason said that was simply his nature, which, of course, should be respected. But shouting gives you presence, which is so important when you're a keeper.

I mentioned earlier the danger of focusing too intensely on the action. Only you can judge the intensity of your concentration, and if you struggle at first, don't worry — it will come good with experience. Keeping your concentration enables you to read the game which, in turn, means you can anticipate a situation rather than reacting once the ball has come your way. If you can visualise what is about to unfold, then you are a step ahead of your opponents. If I see a player making a run to the near post, I can anticipate a cross in that direction and prepare myself accordingly. But if a player runs to the far post, I would hold my position in the belief that the cross would be played there. In other words, being a footballer, especially one with defensive duties, involves watching the players as well as the ball. Anticipation is all-important for a goalkeeper as it can provide you with a precious split-second in which to react.

5

SET-PIECE PLAY

FREE KICKS

Communication skills are especially important in dead-ball situations, because you are responsible for organising your defence, making sure opposing players are well marked and that your teammates are aware of any potential runs into the penalty area.

THE WALL

On free-kicks inside or around the penalty area, a wall is formed to block a direct shot at goal, forcing the kicker to seek an alternative route which, hopefully, you will have covered. It's easier said than done, however, because at international level particularly, there are so many superb strikers of a ball who can make it do all kinds of crazy things and produce shots which are simply impossible to stop. The real free-kick specialists put in hours of work a day to improve their technique and variation, knowing that a successfully flighted one can win a game. In some cases facing a direct free-kick can be as dangerous as facing a penalty.

It is a keeper's job to decide whether to line up a wall, but I don't usually get involved with forming it, neither for Everton nor for Wales. Why? Because if a quick free-kick is taken I risk being caught cold, so I prefer to remain alert and let the defence organise itself in that type of situation. My former manager at Everton, Howard Kendall, put this idea into my head. He said he had seen a game where this had happened and no way did he want a team of his to be caught out like that. If I do want a wall, I have to say how many men should be in it. That depends on the distance and angle of the kick, plus the options available to the kicker. It's better to fill your wall with tall players. In fact, I always try to have our tallest standing on the outside to cut off the top corner of the net. Peter Shreeves, who used to coach Wales, came up

with the idea of having a split wall to ensure a goalkeeper can see the ball. That is, having two small walls, one just behind the other, to cover the whole of the goal. But I'm not too sure about that, and so far it's a tactic I've resisted.

Whatever your decision, it needs to be communicated clearly, and you have to be aware of whether the free-kick is direct or indirect. Once the wall is set up, you must take up a position which covers a ball played over the top of it or around it. There is not much point forming a wall to protect the left of the goal, for example, if you go and stand directly behind it, because that gives the shooter the whole of the right side to aim at. So many goals conceded on free-kicks, as the 1994 World Cup illustrated, can be attributed to a badly formed wall or a keeper taking up a poor position. Ideally, you need courageous players in your wall, because even though many players these days tend to curl the ball, some still prefer a direct blast at goal, which means the people in front, who are supposed to be protecting you, could flinch and suddenly a hole develops in the wall. One tactic which is being increasingly used by goalkeepers on free-kicks within shooting distance is the placing of a defender on each post. This is designed to add cover, the thinking being that shots curled towards the corner of the net, which may be out of the goalkeeper's reach, could be headed clear. This is a useful ploy, although you have to remember that having three players on the goal-line means there is no chance of your opponents being caught offside.

LONG RANGE KICKS

There may not be as much immediate danger from free-kicks beyond shooting range, but that does not mean there is none at all. Balls flighted into the penalty area are always dangerous, which is why marking is so important. Ensure your defenders are on their toes because just a second of ball watching can influence the 90 minutes. The inswinging free-kick from the flanks is becoming increasingly common, where the ball is played into an area which forces keepers to hesitate in coming off their line and where defenders consider it too deep to be their responsibility. The result is often an opponent profiting from the uncertainty to score with a header. So be warned — and be vigilant!

CORNERS

Corners are regarded as a scoring opportunity and must be treated as such by a goalkeeper and his defenders. Again, it's up to you to organise your troops so marking is tight and players are picked up when they make darting runs. Protection of posts is important, so most keepers place players there for extra goal-line cover. How many times have you seen a keeper drop the ball or be beaten by a shot, only for a defender to rescue him by clearing off the line? As with free-kicks, there are many different types of corner, and you have to be prepared for all of them — played short, inswingers, outswingers, balls hit deep or chipped to the near post for a player to head backwards across goal for an attacker to run in and connect. The last of these is a common tactic on corners and is especially difficult to defend against — even though you know what's going to happen. That's why the marking in the box has to be tight.

It is said in all manuals that goalkeepers should adopt a position nearer to the far post on corners because it is easier to run forwards than backwards, should the ball drop out of the desired vicinity. There is some sense in that, but not for me! I've developed my own style, my thinking based on the premise that if I think the ball will be delivered to the near post, why stand at the back? I stand where I think the ball will be flighted, and that's the best advice I can give. Leeds United like using the near post corner

and I remember in one game against them, their giant centre-forward, Lee Chapman, stood at the near post ready to flick on Gordon Strachan's kick. Chapman was marked by one of our players, and all I did was stick my hands up in the air to show Strachan I was there expecting the ball. That forced him either to overhit or underhit his kick, usually the latter, giving my defender the opportunity to head clear. And if he didn't get to the ball, I made sure I did! That said, I have to stress that is *my* style, and I'm fortunate enough to have a reputation which can sometimes intimidate opponents. That isn't so with children. I would advise youngsters — up to the age of 15 — to assume the standard back post position on corners, but after that to try my method and see if it works for them.

Don't stand too far off your line when you expect the ball to swing in, especially if you're playing against the wind. Stand either where your coach has advised or where you feel most comfortable. Keepers should expect to be jostled on corners. Often an opponent will stand right next to you or even on the line, just trying to put you off or impede your run should you intend to come and catch the ball. You can even expect your shirt to be tugged which, considering the number of bodies massed into the area, could go unnoticed by the referee. That's why I don't stand on my line. I don't want to be blocked. But what if an opponent is standing on my goal-line, deliberately blocking my path? The answer is simpler than you may think: just move out from goal. By doing this you give yourself the option of going around either side of him to claim the ball, should it be directed there. The same method can be applied on throw-ins.

THROW-INS

Incredibly, it's not just balls played by feet into the box which are hazardous. Throw-ins can

63

Penalties: don't move too early but always make an attempt

cause as much confusion, panic and danger as corners. If a team has someone with a long throw, they will use him to loft the ball high into the area. Sides like Wimbledon who play to their aerial power thrive on this, and in Vinny Jones they have a player who can gain great distance from the touchline. The tactic on a long throw is similar to that of a corner played to the near post, and so you must defend accordingly. I have my own method of combating this: coming off my line and catching the ball as soon as it's thrown—because the real threat arrives when it's been flicked on. If I can capitalise on my right to use my hands and catch the ball then the danger is over. Logically, if I know to whom the ball will be thrown, then I might as well be next to him with the advantage of using my hands. In the last game of the 1993/94 season when Everton beat Wimbledon 3-2 at Goodison to ensure we remained in the Premiership, people wondered why I always came off my line on long throws, and I was criticised for doing so. Now you know the reason. Okay, so what happens if you're not too good in the air? Well, it's no good hoping the ball doesn't come your way because the chances are it will. Whatever you do, you *must* be positive, so don't be afraid to come. If you do gather, then you will have intimidated your opponents, rather than vice-versa.

PENALTIES

Like it or not, penalties can decide the outcome of matches outside normal time. They are a means of settling even the biggest of tournaments if extra-time has still produced a stalemate, so the stakes can really be high. One thing to bear in mind is that as with a one-on-one situation, the odds are stacked in the favour of the person with the ball. But penalties also provide an opportunity for a goalkeeper to be the hero, as he is not expected to make a save. Having said that, it certainly doesn't mean you shouldn't feel confident. Argentina goalkeeper Sergio Goycoechea made penalty saving something of an art in the 1990 World Cup, and the more he stopped the more the pressure increased on the kickers.

When a spot-kick is awarded it takes time for

the kick to be taken because of the inevitable protests from the penalised team. The longer the delay, the better it is for you. The kicker, aware of the responsibility, wants to get it over with as quickly as possible, and many keepers at senior level apply certain methods of gamesmanship to delay matters even further and make the taker more anxious. I do! It depends on who the referee is, but usually I try to complain just to waste more time. Remember, too, the expectations of the crowd, whether you're playing at international or junior level. For them, the striker should always score. And people can freeze in front of a crowd. . . .

I don't have many hard and fast rules about facing penalties. I just aim to be calm and relaxed. Generally a left footed player with his body to the left of the ball tends to put it to my left, and

if the player is right-footed with his body to the right of the ball, I expect a shot to my right. A straight run-up by a left-footer usually results in a shot to my right, whereas a straight run-up by a right-footed player mainly results in the ball going to my left. Think about it. Anyway, this is only a tip, not a general rule.

Unless I know the kicker — either from previous penalties against me or having watched his style on television — I decide which way I'll dive before the ball is struck. Many keepers actually move *before* the kick is taken. That's not necessarily advantageous because a lot of penalties are drilled at the centre of the goal, and you may just give your opponent an unexpected target in the opposite direction of your dive. Don't move too early but *always* make an attempt.

An ecstatic Sergio Goycoechea of Argentina after saving a vital penalty to beat Yugoslavia in the 1990 World Cup quarter final

6
TRAINING

When the hard work pays off – Everton's FA Cup Final victory celebrations 1984

Thankfully over the last few years, more clubs have placed greater emphasis on goalkeeper training. As you will have gathered, it's something I can't push enough because a player in a specialised position needs specialised training. It's commonsense. In fact, it's always been commonsense, but only recently have clubs shown any. I know, however, that many, if not most, of you won't have the privilege of a goalkeeping coach, but don't worry. You'll do yourself no harm asking friends or teammates to help you with the following drills.

I stress again that the search for perfection can be undertaken by anybody, even keepers at the highest level whom you may feel cannot progress further. But they can. Indeed *everybody* can. That's where training drills and exercises play their part.

As I've already said, if you are willing and you listen, then you will learn and consequently you will improve. Players with more talent may feel they do not have to work as hard as those of less ability, but such a lazy, couldn't-care-less attitude can rebound on them. Training shouldn't be considered as a chore. Sure, it may be hard work and perhaps even monotonous at times, but you must go out to enjoy it, otherwise your will to improve will diminish. The harder you work, the greater your chance of developing, and there are few better feelings than having that work pay off.

THE BASICS

It's important coaches begin with the basics, ensuring their keepers have good hands and

Stances: *Most keepers stances are similar, but none are exactly the same, because of the difference in people's size and weight, as this photograph illustrates. Ideally, the legs should be slightly apart, with the body in what I call the gunslinger pose, as if your hands are about to draw guns from imaginary holsters. The former West Ham and Leeds keeper, Mervyn Day, says your nose should be in front of your toes, meaning your body should be slightly forward. I wouldn't disagree with that.*

the correct stance. After that, they can concentrate on the many particular skills. A goalkeeper's strengths and weaknesses must be assessed, either by himself or by the coach, and naturally the weaknesses demand more work. As at school, where everybody prefers the subjects at which they are good, players like to improve their strengths and can often neglect the weaker aspects of their game. However, you must not only work on what you like, because the rewards will be minimal. The greater your armoury of skills, the better a keeper you are. Trying to improve something at which you are not especially good isn't easy, of course, and there will be times when you feel you are not progressing and your morale drops considerably. But don't give in! If you stick at it, you will see results.

In this section you will see routines to help improve general fitness, incorporating skills which will be required in match situations. I would ask coaches to note that sessions should be balanced, not just concentrated on legwork, and keepers should be aware that some sessions will be easy and others tough. While fitness and basic shot-stopping and handling techniques are essential, I urge you not to neglect your ball skills, especially with the increasing need for goalkeepers to sweep and deal with the ball without using their hands. A good way to improve is to join in your team's five-a-side sessions, as I and many other top-level keepers do.

Many coaching manuals, as I stated early in the book, give a false impression of football. The photographs used to illustrate skills are generally taken on a sunny day, as if Britain never has any rain, wind or snow! Sure, the pictures may look nice, but I'm taking the trouble to tell you now that just because the weather isn't fine on a particular day doesn't mean you shouldn't train. Because matches are played in snow, rain, wind and mud, it stands to reason that you should train in those types of conditions. It may not be pleasant, but it has to be done. Dealing in training with a slippy ball, a hard, icy pitch and a swirling wind, for example, will stand you in good stead come the day you have to play in such conditions. Because you will.

One final thing to remember: just as it's not advisable to have a meal just before playing a match, you shouldn't eat before training unless the food has been properly digested, which takes at least two hours.

So good luck—and good goalkeeping!

WARMING-UP EXERCISES 1 & 2

If you don't stretch before you work or play a game, then you run a high risk of pulling a muscle, which could leave you out of action for weeks. In the photograph above, you can see (*from left to right*) Jason Kearton stretching his shoulders, Stephen Reeves his back, me my sides, Richard Moore and James Speare their shoulders. In the photograph below, Jason is stretching his quads, Stephen his hands, fingers and shoulders, me my groin, Richard his hamstring and James his shoulders. Warm up for at least five minutes.

3 & 4 This exercise, where the ball is passed around the back of the body, enables the keeper to loosen up, while getting used to the feel of the ball. Try this 10 times each side.

5, 6 & 7 More loosening up. Here, the ball is in the hands of a crouching keeper. He flicks it up and moves one of his arms between his legs to catch it as it drops. Try this 10-12 times, alternating the side.

Above: 8 & 9 Another simple exercise with which to warm up. The keeper stands with the ball in his arms and he passes it under one leg and then the other in a fluent motion. Try it 10-12 times.

Below: 10 & 11 A warm-up exercise designed to improve sharpness. The keeper bounces the ball hard in front of him, does a forward roll and catches it before it hits the ground on its way down. Try this five times.

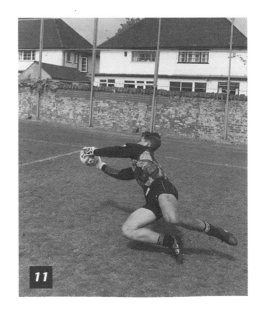

12 A drill to improve speed of thought. Four balls are laid out in a square (north, south, east and west) and two keepers stand in the middle, side by side. One keeper becomes the leader and shouts one of the above directions. The lead keeper dives on the relevant ball, while the second keeper must dive on the ball in the opposite direction. Alternate the leaders and try this 10-12 times.

13 & 14 Four balls are laid in a square, with the keeper starting from a sitting position between two of them. He has to move along the ground sideways to clutch each one in turn as quickly as possible. This exercise simulates the speedy covering of goal from a grounded position, such as reacting to a follow-up shot. Go around the square three times.

15 More speed on the ground. Four balls are laid in a square (north, south, east and west). The keeper stands in the middle, and on the shout of one of the above directions from a colleague, he has to dive on the relevant ball. Try this 10-12 times.

16 & 17 Five balls are placed in a diagonal line, and the keeper has to dive on each one as quickly as possible. This drill is designed to sharpen you up. Go down the line three times.

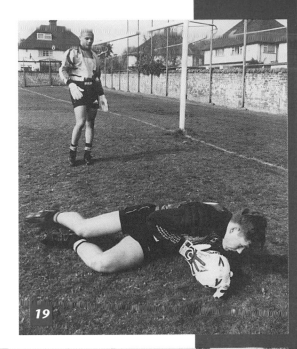

Above: 18 & 19 The server stands three to six yards from the keeper and side-foots the ball through the keeper's legs, forcing him to spin round and dive on the ball. This exercise improves reflexes. Try it 10-12 times, diving on alternate sides.

Right: 20 An exercise to stretch your back, sides and hamstrings. The ball is dropped by the server at the feet of the sitting keeper, making him stretch forward as far as he can. Try this 10-12 times.

27 The server stands a yard from the sitting keeper and throws the ball forward, forcing the keeper to roll back and catch it above his head. This routine stretches the stomach and improves catching ability. Try it 20 times.

Opposite page: 28 & 29 The rowing exercise. The keeper sits with his legs off the ground, ready to catch a ball lobbed by the server, who stands a yard away. On catching it, the keeper returns it immediately, pushing out with both his hands and his feet. This routine, designed to strengthen the stomach and improve ball to eye co-ordination, should be done quickly. Try it 10-12 times.

21, 22 & 23 The server stands between one and two yards from the sitting keeper. He rolls the ball to him quickly on alternate sides, the keeper clutching it and returning it instantly to the server. This is a quick-fire drill, designed to improve catching ability without footwork. Try this 10-12 times, first with the keeper in a sitting position, then kneeling, squatting and finally standing.

24, 25 & 26 The keeper lies flat on his back, with the server standing two yards from his feet. An assistant crouches an arm length away from the keeper, holding a ball. The keeper has to move to that side and touch the ball before sitting up to palm back the ball lobbed by the server, without using his feet. This exercise improves agility, body co-ordination and strengthens wrists and stomach. It should be done as quickly as possible, although it should not be as vigorous with children. Try this 10 times each side.

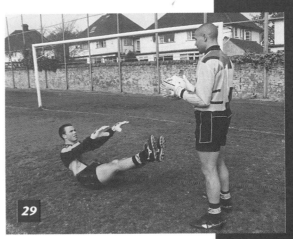

30 The keeper sits up facing the server, who stands two yards away. The server rolls the ball quickly to one side of the keeper, forcing him to move backwards and stop it one-handed. The keeper returns the ball instantly and the drill continues. Not only are the forearms strengthened here, this exercise simulates the occasional need to save shots with only one hand. It should be done on alternate sides, 20 times in total.

Left: 31 This drill strengthens the arms, hands and stomach. The keeper sits facing the server, who is a yard away. The server lobs the ball to the keeper, who must palm it back instantly using only one hand. Try this 10–12 times with each hand.

32 & 33 The keeper adopts a squatting position in goal two yards from the server. The server rolls the ball to alternate sides, forcing the keeper to dive, save and return the ball instantly. Another drill of continuous movement, this improves agility and strength. Note that the keeper must always move forward to attack the ball. Try this 10-12 times.

Below: 34

Another quick-fire exercise. The keeper lies on his stomach, facing a kneeling server, who is two yards away. The server lobs the ball to alternate hands, forcing the keeper to lift his upper body and punch the ball back. A great work out for the back! Try this 20 times in total.

35a

35b

Above: 35a & 35b The server stands four to six yards away from the keeper, who is in a squatting position in goal. The ball is lobbed to alternate sides and the keeper has to save and return it. This is good for thigh muscles, calfs and the stomach. Try this 10-12 times.

Below: 36a & 36b Note the small goals in this exercise, which improves agility. The server, who is six yards from goal, kicks the ball to alternate sides, forcing the keeper to save from a kneeling position. Remember, always attack the ball — never go back! Try this 10-12 times.

36a

36b

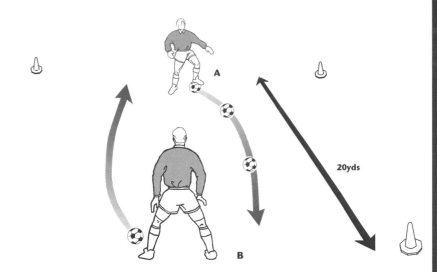

20yds

Above: Similar to a warm-up exercise used on the pitch. Players **A** and **B** are both keepers, standing in goals defined by cones, which are the width of a normal goal. Each keeper has to score, first by throwing the ball past his opponent as fast as possible, using the right and left hands. Then try kicking the ball, starting with a volley (both feet) and then a half-volley. Then progress by introducing a striker to score from any rebounds. After that, remove the striker, but add two players, six-yards away from the keeper at each end. Their job is to deflect the ball, get in its line and generally distract the keeper. Next, reduce the goals to five-a-side size, reduce the size of the pitch and have the keepers kneeling, trying to score by throwing the ball in the opposite goal. Finally, as above, only with the keepers adopting a sitting position. Each exercise should be comprised of 10-12 throws/shots.

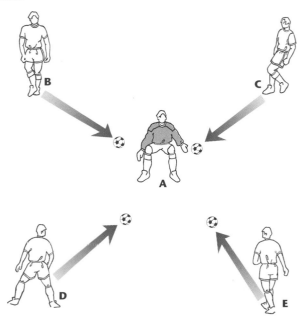

Left:
The goalkeeper stands in the middle of a square of four colleagues, who are six yards away. In turn, they each punt a ball at him, and he moves around the square to save. This is an exercise to develop handling and footwork. Try going three times round the square.

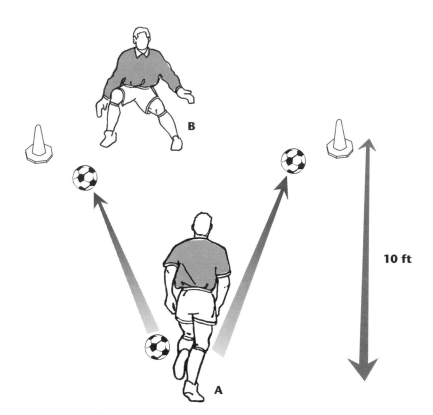

Left: Keeper **B** stands in a goal marked out by two cones (half the size of a full goal), while server **A** stands 10 feet away. The server kicks the ball low towards goal, obliging the keeper to save. He returns the ball to the server, who makes it dead and shoots again. Try this 10-12 times.

10 ft

Right: Servers **A** and **B** stand 10 yards either side of keeper **C**. The keeper faces server **A**, who kicks the ball through the keeper's legs to server **B**. Server **B** kicks the ball back first time forcing the keeper to turn around sharply and save. The keeper returns the ball to server **B**, who begins the action again. Try this 10-12 times.

10 yds   10 yds

10 yds   10 yds

37 The server stands on the six-yard line, with two balls in his hands and two at his feet. He can choose to throw or kick one at the keeper, who must save from a standing position in goal. This is a reflex-tester. Try it with 8 or 12 balls.

38 & 39 A real test of speed off the ground. The server stands four to six yards from the keeper, and throws the ball to one side. The keeper has to dive, catch the ball, return it and be ready to dive immediately to the same side again. This is a rapid-fire drill, and you should try it with six lobs each side.

40 The server stands six yards from goal, while the keeper lies flat on his stomach along the goal-line, his outstretched arms level with a post. After shouting "Go!" the server lobs the ball to the unguarded area of the net, high or low, and the keeper has to either catch it or knock it away. This exercise is all about covering distance with speed. It's as if you were positioned at the near post for a cross which was played unexpectedly to the far post, and you had to make up the ground quickly. Try this 10 times.

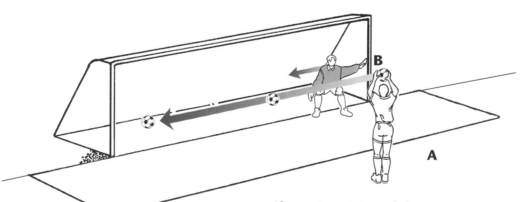

Above: A variation of the exercise 40, with the keeper **B** touching his left post, while server **A** stands in the centre of the goal around the six-yard line. On shouting "Go!" the server lobs the ball towards the far post, with the keeper having to scramble across to save. Try this five times from each side.

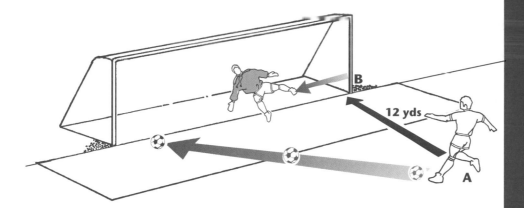

Above: Another variation, only this time server **A** stands 12 yards from goal, opposite the keeper **B**, who is touching his left post. On a command, the server fires the ball towards the far post, and the keeper must attempt to save. Because the ball is kicked in this drill, it is harder than the previous one. Try it five times from each side.

41 & 42 Note the small goal (*from the post to the marker on the keepers right*). The keeper is kneeling on the goal-line, while a colleague stands six yards away to side-foot a volley lobbed by the server. This tests the keeper's reflexes, ability to watch the ball, and bravery. The goal can be extended to two-thirds of the full size when the keeper is standing. Try each exercise 10-12 times.

43, 44 & 45 A similar exercise to the previous one. Here, there are two small coned goals, each with a kneeling keeper. A server stands outside the "field," where he lobs to a colleague, who volleys at either goal, forcing the keeper to save. Tests reflexes and concentration. Try this 10-12 times.

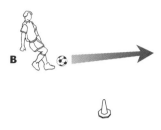

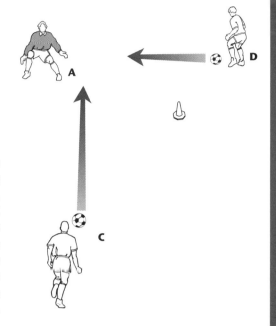

Above: A is the keeper standing to protect three goals, six to eight feet wide, defined by the cones. Servers **B**, **C** and **D** stand 12 yards away, with **C** firing the ball at the relevant goal. Once saved, **A** must turn to his left to save from **D**, and then he must move to his left again to face **B**'s shot. Servers must make sure the keeper is in a set position before shooting. Try this with each server firing five balls.

46 & 47 The keeper stands upright, four to six yards away from two colleagues, each with a ball in their hands. One player rolls the ball to the keeper, and on rolling it back to the server, the other player lobs the ball high, forcing the keeper to jump and catch. This exercise improves reactions, spring and co-ordination. Try it 10 or 12 times.

48, 49 & 50 The keeper stands on the goal-line with his back to play. Behind him on the six-yard line are four servers, each holding a ball. One of the servers shouts — indicating he is about to shoot — and the keeper instantly spins around, attempting to save. This drill is about awareness, eye to ball co-ordination and reflexes. Try this with eight balls in total.

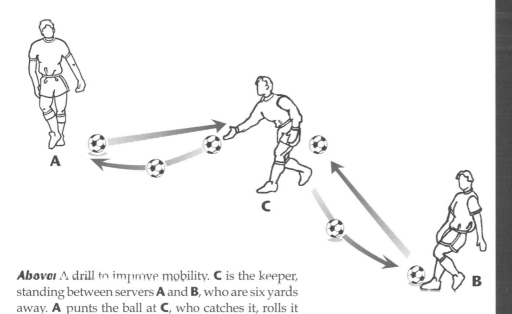

Above: A drill to improve mobility. **C** is the keeper, standing between servers **A** and **B**, who are six yards away. **A** punts the ball at **C**, who catches it, rolls it back instantly and turns around to do the same from **B**. This exercise should be done quickly. Try it 10–12 times.

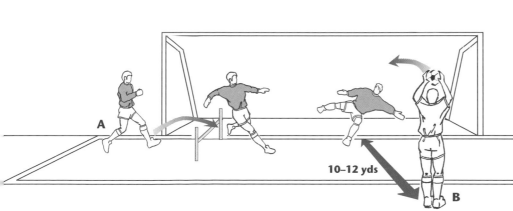

10–12 yds

Above: An exercise designed to improve spring. **A** is the keeper, who stands on the end of the six-yard box, while a pole balanced two feet off the ground, or between two cones, is placed in the goal area. The keeper must leap over the pole and then, on landing, spring up to catch a lobbed ball from server **B**, who is standing 10–12 yards from the goal-line. Try this five times from each side.

51, 52 & 53 A cone placed five-yards from a goalpost makes a small goal. The keeper stands next to the post and on a command he has to run to touch the cone. On sprinting back towards the post, the server lobs the ball towards the un-guarded area, forcing the keeper to save. This drill is designed to improve agility and leg-speed. Try it 10–12 times.

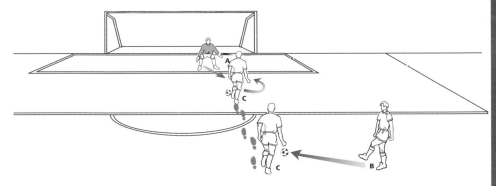

Above: Server **B** stands outside the penalty area and plays the ball to server **C**, who is also outside. Server **C** advances into the area and tries to dribble the keeper. An exercise all about timing, bravery and decision-making. Try this five times.

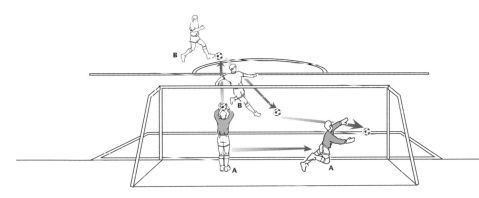

Above: Server **B** stands outside the penalty area and receives the ball from keeper **A**. The server plays the ball into the area and attempts to score by either dribbling the keeper or shooting first time. This improves awareness. Try it five times.

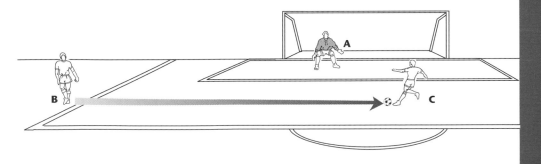

Above: An exercise in shot-stopping. Server **B** stands outside the penalty area and crosses the ball low for striker **C**, who runs in and shoots first time. The keeper has to adjust his position and save. Try it 10-12 times.

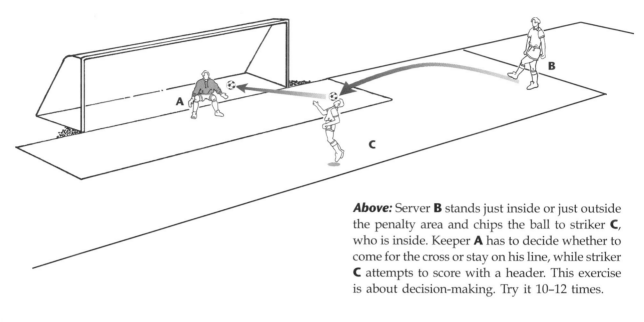

Above: Server **B** stands just inside or just outside the penalty area and chips the ball to striker **C**, who is inside. Keeper **A** has to decide whether to come for the cross or stay on his line, while striker **C** attempts to score with a header. This exercise is about decision-making. Try it 10–12 times.

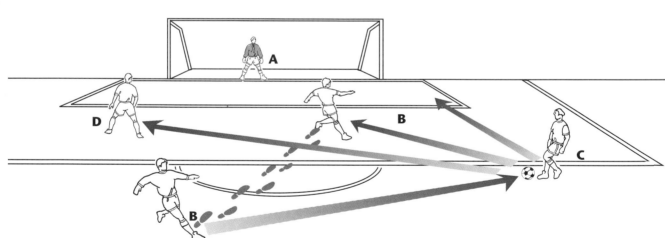

Above: Another drill which improves decision-making and alertness. Server **B** stands outside the penalty area and plays the ball to player **C**, who is just inside or just outside it. Player **C** can choose whether to pass to player **B**, who has run into the area, or to player **D**, who is also inside. Alternatively, player **C** can opt to shoot at goal. The keeper has to be prepared for three alternatives. Try this 10–12 times.

54, 55, & 56
For better leg-speed. Ten cones are placed in a zig-zag line. The keeper or keepers have to run down that line as quickly as possible, touching each cone. Try it three times.

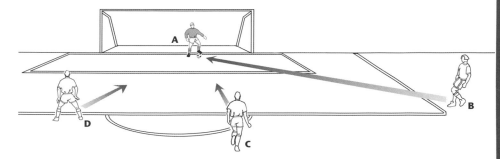

Above: More footwork, but this time with a ball. Server **B** plays the part of a defender, standing outside the area. Player **D** is also a defender, whose presence offers keeper **A** a solution if required. Server **B** kicks the ball to the keeper, as if it were a backpass, while striker **C** rushes in to close him down. The keeper must clear the ball safely with his feet, either by going for distance or attempting to find player **D**. He cannot use server **B**! This exercise can be made more difficult through the presence of another striker. Try it 10 times.

57, 58 & 59 This is a real pressure exercise! The keeper stands on his goal-line, facing a server on the six-yard line, who has at least four balls at his disposal. The server throws the ball anywhere at the goal, forcing the keeper to save. As the keeper lands, the server throws another ball goalwards, and the routine continues. Try it 10 times.

60 & 61 Another pressure exercise. A cone is placed eight yards from goal. On a command, the keeper has to run off the goal-line, touch the cone and run back to his line. As he does so, the server, standing three yards from the cone, lobs the ball goalwards *(continued over)*

62

63

62 & 63 *(continued from previous page)* The keeper has to try and knock it over the bar. The keeper must keep his eye on the ball in this drill, which is also designed to improve spring. Try this 10 times using different hands to save.

Above: A variation of the previous exercise. Keeper **A** stands outside the box, while server **B** stands on the penalty spot facing the goal. The keeper runs towards the server, crawls through his legs, and after doing so, the server lobs the ball goalwards. The keeper then has to leap from a grounded position to save. Try it 10 times using different hands to save.

QUICK & SIMPLE EXERCISES

Here are a few quick and simple exercises, most of which have variations. Of course, you do not have to do each one the suggested number of times. It depends on your ability, your age, your level of fitness, your time and also your desire. To non-professionals, my advice to you is to start slowly and gradually build up your work-rate. Attempting to complete each one to the full from scratch is not advisable, as you risk suffering injury and exhaustion. Choose the drills you require. Basically, just be sensible.

EXERCISE 1

a) The keeper sits facing the server, who rolls the ball along the ground to the keeper's right. The keeper has to stretch and catch the ball two-handed and return it as he comes back into an upright position. While upright, the server then rolls the ball to the keeper's left. This drill can also be done from a kneeling, squatting and standing position. Do this 10-12 times each side.

b) As above, but this time the server throws the ball at shoulder height, rather than rolling it.

c) As above, except that the keeper catches the ball with one hand (right then left), firstly on the ground and then in the air.

EXERCISE 2

a) The keeper sits facing three servers, who each have a ball. Server one rolls it to the keeper's right, where he has to catch it two-handed before returning it on coming back upright. On doing so, server two then throws the ball above the keeper's head, and after returning it, server three then rolls the ball to the keeper's left, which he must catch two-handed. This drill can also be performed from a kneeling, squatting and standing position. Do all three saves six times.

b) As above, except that the ball is thrown in the air.

EXERCISE 3

a) The keeper sits facing the server, who throws the ball above the keeper's head, forcing him to move backwards and catch two-handed. The keeper returns the ball, keeping his feet on the ground at all times. This drill can also be performed when kneeling, squatting and standing. Do each one six times.

b) As above, but this time as soon as the keeper has returned the ball, the server drops it at his feet. The keeper must reach down and catch it two-handed, keeping his feet on the ground.

EXERCISE 4

a) The keeper sits facing the server. A ball is placed an arm's length away from the keeper's right. He has to reach over and touch that ball one-handed. On coming back upright, the server lobs another ball above his head, which must be knocked back with the left hand. This exercise can also be done with the keeper kneeling, squatting and standing. Do each one six times.

b) As above, but change sides.

EXERCISE 5

The keeper sits facing the server, who drops a ball at arms length around the keeper's body. He must stretch to catch it before returning it to the server. Do this 10 times.

EXERCISE 6

The keeper sits on the goal-line facing play between two lines of balls, an arm's length apart each side and spaced at two-yard intervals up to the edge of the penalty area. The keeper has to dive on every ball (right and left), working down the line without his backside leaving the ground. This is a shuffle movement, designed to improve body speed without the significant use of legs. Do this one or two times.

EXERCISE 7

a) The keeper sits facing a server, while a second server stands between two and five yards behind the keeper. The facing server rolls the ball to the keeper's right for him to catch one-handed and to return it. The keeper then spins around to face the second server, who throws the ball again to the keeper's right for the action to be repeated. This routine can also be performed from a kneeling, squatting and standing position. Do it 10 times.

b) As above, but test the keeper's left.

c) As above, except that the keeper must knock the ball away one-handed along the ground.

d) As above, except that the keeper must knock the ball away one-handed in the air.

e) As above, except that the keeper must catch the ball two-handed in the air.

EXERCISE 8

The keeper sits facing the server, who lobs the ball at different heights and angles, forcing the keeper to punch it away one-handed using his own power rather than the pace of the ball for momentum. Vary the hands. This drill can also be performed from a kneeling, squatting and standing position. Do this 10-12 times.

EXERCISE 9

a) The keeper sits facing the server, who lobs the ball above his head and above arms length. The keeper must therefore stretch and catch the ball two-handed before returning it. This can also be done with the keeper kneeling, squatting and standing. Do this 10-12 times.

b) As above, except that the keeper tips the ball away one-handed.

EXERCISE 10

a) Make a triangle with cones, discs or balls, three yards apart, to form three goals. A server stands opposite each goal, eight yards away. The keeper stands next to one of the cones, and on a command the first server will throw or kick the ball along the ground just inside the first cone to the keeper's left. The keeper must dive on the ball before it enters the goal. Upon returning it to the first server, the second server plays the next ball in to the keeper's left and so on. Go around the triangle six times on your left side and six times on your right.

b) As above, but the servers play the ball in the air.

c) As above, but the servers play the ball along the ground for the keeper to knock away one-handed.

d) As above, but the servers play the ball in the air for the keeper to knock away one-handed.

e) As above, but the servers can play the ball in at any height for the keeper to catch or knock away.

f) As above, but the servers must let the keeper set himself in the middle of the goal, and balls can be played in at any side and at any height.